A DETECTION OF THE TRINITY

A DETECTION
OF THE
TRINITY

John Thurmer
Chancellor of Exeter Cathedral

EXETER
THE PATERNOSTER PRESS

AUSTRALIA
Bookhouse Australia Ltd.,
P.O. Box 115, Flemington Markets, NSW 2129

SOUTH AFRICA
Oxford University Press,
P.O. Box 1141, Cape Town

British Library Cataloguing in Publication Data

Thurmer, John
    A detection of the Trinity.
    1. Trinity
    I. Title
    231'.044   BT111.2

ISBN 0-85364-395-4

Typeset in Great Britain by
Busby Typesetting & Design, 52 Queen Street, Exeter, Devon
and printed for The Paternoster Press,
Paternoster House, 3 Mount Radford Crescent, Exeter, Devon
by A. Wheaton & Co. Ltd., Exeter, Devon.

Contents

Preface

In the small Essex town where I spent my youth Dorothy
L. Sayers lived a few doors away. Like a local stately home
or national monument, she was usually taken for granted,
though occasionally she was an object of interest or
amusement when she did battle with the Vicar, the press or
local tradespeople. Whether her proximity encouraged me
to read her books I cannot remember, but read them I did,
and the religious writings before the detection. I learnt
most of my theology first from her, and then I later re-
learnt it from more conventional authorities. This little
book which explores her insight into the central Christian
doctrine of the Trinity is a recognition of what I (and no
doubt others) owe to her.

Readers may wonder whether this work is supposed to
be 'academic' or 'devotional'. I hope it is both. I have no
doubt that the analogy of the Trinity might be the subject
of much weightier writing, and I hope it will be. But prayer
and study ought to go together; Christian doctrine
belongs, if not to the natural man, at least to the common
man, and not only to the scholar. Religious doctrines
which can be understood only by experts are not worth
much. I have tried to write for the common man, and have
put the more technical material in the footnotes.

I owe a great debt to the Rev. Douglas Powell, formerly
Senior Lecturer in Theology in the University of Exeter,
who put his time and his learning at my disposal, subjected
my ideas to criticism and opened for me new areas of
thought. He will not be satisfied with what I have written,
and should not be held responsible for it, but much of it is
due to him. For their encouragement I must thank also
Archbishop Michael Ramsey and the Rev. Dr. Paul Avis;
and Janet Stiling and Hilary Tolley of the Department of
History and Archaeology in the University of Exeter, who
typed the manuscript.

Introduction

Nothing is more distinctive of Christianity than its doctrine that God is a Trinity in Unity, Father, Son and Holy Spirit, 'three Persons and one God'. Through the centuries the doctrine has been violently attacked and robustly defended. Alternative interpretations of the Bible, like Judaism and Islam, themselves great world religions, deny it, as do popular modern deviations and vociferous Christian radicals, to say nothing of scornful unbelievers. Much Christian acceptance of the doctrine has been puzzled or lukewarm. Some clergymen dread preaching on Trinity Sunday, and their feeling is no doubt shared by their hearers. But the difficulty is not limited to special days or rare occasions. Christian thought, speech and worship are saturated with the Trinity. Psalms and canticles end with the doxology, 'Glory be to the Father, and to the Son, and to the Holy Ghost', and many hymns conclude with a metrical version of it. Sometimes this includes technical terms of trinitarian theology like 'consubstantial, co-eternal'.[1] Baptism is explicitly, and all Christian activity implicitly, 'in the name of the Father, and of the Son, and of the Holy Ghost'.

---

1. For consideration of these terms, see Chapters 3 and 7.

Worshippers who valiantly try to make the language meaningful easily fall into one or other of the two main mistakes—having the One at the expense of the Three, or having the Three at the expense of the One. In the first case, Father, Son and Spirit become labels for particular forms, appearances or 'modes' of God's Being, when there may be other labels and appearances, perhaps without number. This deprives the trinitarian words of both uniqueness and authority. Such a line of thought may be called 'modalist' or 'Sabellian'—after Sabellius, a theologian of the early third century. Sabellius was accused of this particular deviation, and his name is commonly used to describe it.[2] In the second case, Father, Son and Spirit are three separate Gods—'tritheism'—a contradiction of the central doctrine of the Bible and a move back towards paganism. If three, why not more?

The ease with which human thought slides towards these two unacceptable extremes might encourage a radical rejection of the idea of the Trinity. Anyone disposed to such a rejection has at hand two large-scale non-trinitarian versions of biblical religion, namely, post-Christian Judaism and Islam. It is clearly beyond the scope of a study like this to evaluate other faiths. But it may be noted how often, in the modern western world, Judaism becomes a cultural attitude which is religiously either agnostic or atheist. Moslem leaders officially 'stopped thinking' in the twelfth century[3], and the ability of Islam to stand up to the corrosive influence of western thought must be regarded as highly doubtful. Christian attempts to abandon the Trinity have not been successful either. There is a 'Unitarian' chapel a few hundred yards from my study, but it has long been little more than a historic monument. The anti-Trinitarianism of certain academic theologians such as

2. Persons in the early church who are associated with particular 'heresies' did not necessarily teach what their names are used to describe. Often, as with Sabellius, it is now difficult or impossible to discover exactly what they *did* teach.

3. The effect of the enormously influential teaching of Al Ghazali (born 1085) was to reject reason as a guide either in religion or in the affairs of this world.

G.W.H. Lampe, Maurice Wiles and Don Cupitt is like the ultra-scepticism of some New Testament scholars, a 'sickness that destroyeth in the noon-day'. Mainstream Christianity, Eastern and Western, Catholic and Protestant, cleaves to the Trinity.

But it often seems to do so almost without knowing why. For some it is enough that 'the Church teaches' (as it certainly does). For others, it is 'what the Bible teaches', (though the doctrine of the Trinity is not, in any developed and explicit form, found in the Bible). In either case, we are told, in effect, 'Don't expect to understand; just accept it.' This attitude can be illustrated from the life and work of K.E. Kirk, Bishop of Oxford from 1937 to 1954. Kirk was a distinguished trinitarian scholar, and a persuasive and imaginative preacher. But he had no expectation that the doctrine of the Trinity would appeal to either the minds or the hearts of believers. It simply had to be accepted on authority.

Now however necessary the element of authority in such a matter, it seems likely that the doctrine of the Trinity, if it is true, must be acceptable, even attractive, to devout intelligence and imagination. The teaching of Jesus combined a distinctive note of authority with a wide-ranging use of human observation and experience as providing either a correspondence with, or a contrast to, the things of God. In either case, human thought and feeling are used and appealed to.

But *what*, in human thought or experience, can God the Holy Trinity be like? Answering that question is the business of this book, and calls for the use of materials ranging over three thousand years. But the confidence that the question is worth asking, and is, in principle, *answerable*, comes from a source at first sight surprising, the modern detective novelist Dorothy L. Sayers (1893-1957). Her book *The Mind of the Maker* is unique in being a developed and confident appeal to something in human experience corresponding to, or providing a direct analogy of, the Holy Trinity. Because of that this present book is called a Detection. Not, as Sayers would have been the first to agree, that the Trinity is like one of her detective problems. For such detective problems exist only in the mind of their maker, and so are completely soluble. That is why they are such good escapist literature. The Trinity is not a problem but a mystery—something beyond and outside us, yet inviting exploration. It is more like a 'problem' in real life, where detection is still appropriate, but where it leaves loose ends and continuing mystery.

The chapters which follow do not set out to be a systematic study of the doctrine of the Trinity, or the history of its development. There is no intention here of retelling the great story of the formulation of the Christian mind on the matter in the early centuries of the Church, and some of the greatest thinkers and most famous events go unnoticed. The doctrine has, however, acquired a formidable range of technical terms which cannot be ignored. To some these are a repulsive jargon, to others a delicate instrument in the service of the highest of human thoughts. I try, in either the text or the footnotes, to provide some explanation of such terms for non-specialists. In fact, a great deal of this book is about the meaning of words, as is appropriate for a study inspired by a professional writer whose business was words.

Our main enquiry, however, does not begin with Sayers. It begins, as the King in *Alice in Wonderland* advised, 'at the beginning', so that we may detect some of the background of the Sayers doctrine. Where, from our point of view, is 'the beginning'? The beginning is the words we use, and the first significant use of them, in the early books of the Bible. These will turn out to be much more 'trinitarian' than is commonly thought—not that they contain statements like the Athanasian creed—but because they supply the language and the presuppositions out of which the doctrine was fashioned. God does nothing suddenly or without preparation.

But if there is a satisfactory analogy of the Trinity, why does it not appear until the twentieth century? That, too, needs an answer, but it is an answer which will emerge from the exploration of the analogy. The ability of Christianity to be continually fruitful in thought may be a fulfilment of Our Lord's promise, 'Greater works than these you will do, because I go to the Father.'

CHAPTER ONE

Meaning and Analogy

How shall we speak of God? Can we speak of him at all?
To this second question certain modern philosophers
would answer 'No'. For, they hold, human language is
useful or meaningful only if it is about physical things
discernible by our senses.[1] Many who are not philosophers
may ask, of theologians' statements about God, 'How do
they know?'—a question which expects the answer, 'They
do not.' But this sort of agnosticism, however under-
standably provoked by theological know-alls, is often used
very selectively, to discredit doctrines we do not like.

Human language has always dealt with many things not
directly perceived by our senses. If it did not, it would be
impoverished beyond recognition, and would exhibit
'1984' characteristics—'Every year fewer and fewer words,
with the range of consciousness always a little smaller.'
'There will be no thought as we understand it now.'[2]

1. The French thinker Auguste Comte (1798-1857) confined intellectual
   enquiry to observable ('positive') facts; hence 'Positivism'. The
   modern form of this, 'Logical Positivism', owes much to Ludwig
   Wittgenstein (1889-1951) and A.J. Ayer (b.1910).
2. George Orwell, *Nineteen eighty-four*, 1949.

When we speak of anything not directly accessible to the
senses, we use some sort of comparison, direct or implied,
with what is so accessible. Such a comparison would be
technically described as a metaphor or an analogy. Many
of these have become so common and widespread that it
requires considerable effort to realise that they *are*
analogies. 'Do you see?' says the teacher, after explaining
something to his pupils. But the *seeing* here is metaphorical. There is an implied comparison between seeing
something physical and understanding a proposition. Even
'understanding' is metaphorical!

When one comes to something like the economy, that
god of this world which rules our lives, analogies abound.
'Wine-lakes' and 'butter mountains' placard their nature as
analogies. But something much more commonplace like
'inflation' is the same. The process whereby you need
more and more money at face value to provide the same
purchasing power is compared (presumably) to the way a
balloon is blown up—it gets bigger and bigger, but it is still
the same amount of rubber. He would be a bold man who
claimed that, because 'inflation' is an analogy, it therefore
did not mean anything or could not be 'true'.

Human language describes God, or the gods, by means
of analogies with earthly beings and experiences. The Bible
accepts and controls such language. God is invisible spirit
and therefore not to be identified with any idol. He is one
and not many, so not to be described as a family or community like that of Mount Olympus. He made man in his
image, and is therefore to be described as a man; but he is
not man as we are man; he is not bound by birth and
death; he is not sinful and vacillating.

'For my thoughts are not your thoughts,
Neither are your ways my ways', says the Lord.
'For as the heavens are higher than the earth,
So are my ways higher than your ways
And my thoughts than your thoughts' (Isaiah 55:8,9.)

Just as the Bible does not argue about God's existence,
but assumes it, and is concerned to exhibit his character, so

it does not discuss the general use of analogy. It assumes the human analogy and defines and extends it in ways discussed in chapters 2-5. These ways are distinct, and in some sense disparate, but they all contribute to the trinitarian analogy—that is, that God and man are each a trinity, and to learn about one is to learn about the other.

Analogy does not, in the scientific or mathematical sense, *prove* the truth of a proposition. If I show an analogy between the trinitarian nature of God and the trinitarian nature of man, and the analogy is allowed to be valid and plausible, I have not thereby 'proved' the Trinity. We walk by faith, not by sight, and the creeds are not logical deductions from observable phenomena. If they were we would have no freedom. What the analogy does is to show you where to look if you want your faith to find intellectual and rational expression. The analogy of the Trinity indicates, if its validity is admitted, that the doctrine of the Trinity is *not nonsense*; for on a different scale it shows the same pattern of three-in-one existing in man, in oneself. This is proof, not as demonstrating logical necessity, but in the older sense of 'testing' the idea against experience and authority.[3]

To some believers the prominence of analogy in speaking of God is disappointing. Ought we not, they feel, to be able to speak of God with a more direct assurance? What defence have we got against unbelievers like Feuerbach (the teacher, in this matter, of the gurus of the modern world, Marx and Freud) who held for example that, because the ancient Israelites gave great authority to human fathers, so they came to postulate a 'father in heaven'?

As we have seen, many areas of human life, as well as religion, use analogy, and without it human language as

3. This sense of 'prove' is common in the English of the 1611 ('Authorized') version of the Bible. David, rejecting Saul's armour, said, 'I cannot go with these, for I have not proved them.' (1 Samuel 17:39). 'Prove all things; hold fast that which is good. Abstain from all appearance of evil.' (I Thessalonians 5:21,22). It also makes the best sense of the adage 'The Church to teach, the Bible to prove' popularized by Edward Hawkins's sermon on Tradition, 1818.

we understand it would not survive. Biblical analogies are certainly not the crude transference of an earthly to a heavenly reality, as the unbelievers of modern Europe suppose. They are controlled and limited, and they work both ways. If the Bible sees a certain correspondence between God and a human father (or king or judge or shepherd) this may indeed teach us about God. But it teaches us also about man, and how man in these various capacities should behave.[4]

Finally, God (as we may say) accepts the criticism that analogy is not enough. In our first detailed piece of Bible study (chapter 2) we are introduced to God giving himself human expression. The heart of the Christian faith is that God has *become* man; accepting birth and death; and making himself as knowable and describable as anyone in human history. But the incarnation does not do away with analogy. On the contrary; it 'proves', in the sense of testing and confirming, the human analogy of God.[5]

4. 'While according to the analogy of being, fatherhood is one of the most significant analogies that human experience affords to describe God, Barth would assert that, on the contrary, God has graciously conferred upon human paternity certain attributes that reflect his own eternal and perfect fatherhood.' (Paul Avis, 'Karl Barth: The Reluctant Virtuoso', in *Theology*, May 1983.) As the writer of the article says, Barth's reaction to liberalism and unbelief is important, but by itself it is an inadequate view of analogy.
5. For a tendency in theologians to use the language of analogy without admitting or recognizing it, see J.A. Thurmer, 'The Analogy of the Trinity', in the *Scottish Journal of Theology* Vol. 34, pp.509-515.

CHAPTER TWO

Angel of the Presence

'And the angel of the LORD appeared to Moses in a
flame of fire out of the midst of a bush ... and he said,
"I am the God of your father..." And Moses hid his
face, for he was afraid to look at God' (Exodus 3:2,6).

It is an odd thing for the angel to say. We would expect
him to say, 'The God of your father has sent me', or words
to that effect. Instead, he says, 'I am the God of your
father'. It seems that when Yahweh[1] wishes to communicate with men, he does so by manifesting himself as an
'angel'; or, in one case (Genesis 19) as two angels; in
another (Genesis 18) as 'three men'. These persons are in
fact Yahweh himself. They speak as God, and are called so
by men. Even when there are two or three, they are
addressed as 'Thou'. Their human form causes them to be

1. So modern scholars transliterate the divine name, which since the
sixteenth century has been familiar as Jehovah. For centuries before
the Christian era it was too holy to be spoken, the reader substi-
tuting the title 'Lord' (Hebrew *Adonai*, Greek *Kyrios*), and many
modern translations represent it by LORD. It presents the modern
speaker or writer with a dilemma; for while Yahweh is unfamiliar
and Jehovah inaccurate, the substitution of the title LORD for the
personal name spoils the flavour of the Old Testament, much as the
omission of the name Jesus would affect the New.

spoken of as men. They speak and are understood. They
eat (Genesis 18). Jacob wrestles with one (Genesis 32). But
evidently their human form is transient. The visitor to
Samson's parents, identified by them as God, went back to
heaven in the flame of sacrifice (Judges 13:20).

To communicate with man, therefore, Yahweh manifests
himself in human form—usually as one man, sometimes
more; but if more than one, the delegation is a unity. On
the threshold of scripture God is so portrayed—not
occasionally, but consistently, in his dealings with
Abraham, Jacob, Moses, Joshua and the Judges. At least
fifteen examples of this usage can be found.[2]

So if we think there are no clues to the doctrine of the
Trinity in the Old Testament (as is commonly said, by
both friends and enemies) we are certainly mistaken. The
God of the Old Testament, Yahweh, is a being of 'complex
simplicity',[3] of unity-in-distinction, and this is the basis of
both the Incarnation and the Trinity. The angel of Yahweh
'is God in human form—the ancients even spoke of a doctrine of two natures! ... The figure of the angel of the Lord
has conspicuous Christological qualities. ... He is a type, a
"shadow" of Jesus Christ.'[4]

It is easy to see, however, why we do not confidently
appeal to 'the angel of Yahweh' as an Old Testament clue
to the characteristic Christian doctrines. To western man
today, and for centuries past, 'angel' means a non-human
created being, preferably with wings. We may, or may
not, think that such beings have any real existence. But if
they have, they are created beings, *creatures*, and this
makes them worse than useless as precursors of the divine

2. They are conveniently listed in G.A.F. Knight, *A Biblical
   Approach to the Doctrine of the Trinity*, Oliver and Boyd, 1953,
   pp.25-26, and *A Christian Theology of the Old Testament*, SCM,
   2nd Ed. 1964, pp.70-73. His conclusions are disappointingly
   negative.

3. The expression, not originally applied directly to God, is R.C.
   Moberly's, in his Oxford University Sermon, *A Religious View of
   Human Personality*, 1902, in *Problems and Principles*, Murray,
   1909, p.62. It is a fitting summary of his analogy of the Trinity; see
   below, chapters 7 and 8.

4. Gerhard von Rad, *Genesis—A Commentary*, SCM, E.T. 1963.

persons of the Trinity. If the Son and the Spirit are 'angels' in this sense, then the doctrine of the Trinity has gone, as in ancient Christian deviations like Islam and modern ones like Jehovah's Witnesses.

But in the Bible 'angel' does not mean (or does not *solely* mean) a 'non-human created being'. It means a messenger, and as such it can be applied to human nature, supernatural created nature or divine nature. Of itself it does not describe nature at all, but function. In this it is parallel to Spirit, which can also be applied to men, to non-human created beings, good or bad, and to God.

The conflict about the meaning of the word 'Angel' is well illustrated by Isaiah 63:9: 'The angel of his (God's) presence saved them.' Here, as in the visitation of the patriarchs, the Angel is God himself. The Hebrew word translated 'presence' is, literally, 'face'; as Jacob said after he had wrestled with the Angel, 'I have seen God face to face' (Genesis 32:30). But in the Greek Bible the text was amended to make 'angel' mean a subordinate or created being. This is the version chosen, without even a marginal reading, in the New English Bible: 'It was no envoy, no angel, but he himself that delivered them.' In giving its support to this limitation of the meaning of 'angel' NEB is continuing a long process, but its support is none the less regrettable.

Jesus himself appealed to relatively unfamiliar parts of the Old Testament to support his teaching. In his recorded words he does not describe himself as the angel of Yahweh; perhaps that would have been uncharacteristically self-regarding. But the early church certainly did.[5] The extent to which it drew on angelology for its doctrine of the Trinity has been obscured, and still is obscured, by later Christian presuppositions. In fact, 'Logos' ('Word') Christology is often more correctly called 'Angel' Christology, for the Logos is manifested as an angel, usually the Archangel Michael, with Gabriel as the Holy Spirit (though for some Gabriel is the Logos).[6] Origen interpreted the seraphim of Isaiah's vision as the Son and the Holy Spirit glorifying the Father.[7] Irenaeus[8] does the same. The Shepherd of Hermas, that nearly-canonical work contained in the

Codex Sinaiticus, has an elaborate angelic Trinitarianism.

In one place, and that a unique and important one, this usage survives to this day in western Christianity. The Roman Canon of the Mass is a prayer of great antiquity, and until the recent revisions was the central prayer of every Roman Catholic mass (apart from those of the Eastern Uniat churches). This prayer compares the consecrated Bread and Wine to the sacrifices of Abel, Abraham and Melchisedek, and then prays that they may be 'brought by the hands of thy holy Angel to thine altar on high'. The holy Angel is Christ himself, who presents the Church's gifts to the Father. But this interpretation is frequently obscured or denied. For centuries the Canon was said silently and its details made little impact. And it is noteworthy that in the modern alternatives to the Canon the Angel does not appear.

In the east the Trinity as three angels appearing to Abraham is a common icon.[9] But with the exception noted above this usage is unknown in the west, where the use of

5. Tertullian provides a neat definition: '[The Son] has been called "Angel of great counsel", that is, messenger (*nuntius*) a term expressive of official function, not of nature ... I may then more easily say ... that the Son is actually an angel, that is, a messenger from the Father, than that there is an angel in the Son'. (*De carne Christi* XIV). Tertullian held that (non-human created) angels could assume temporary human form, without birth or death, and the Son prepared for his full incarnation as man by participating in this exercise. 'The Lord himself ... appeared to Abraham amongst those angels without being born ... Christ ... was even then rehearsing how to converse with, and liberate, and judge the human race, in the habit of a flesh which as yet was not born because it did not yet mean to die' (*De carne Christi* VI).
6. See J. Daniélou, *The Theology of Jewish Christianity*, Darton, Longman and Todd, E.T. 1964, chapter 4, 'The Trinity and Angelology'.
7. *Questions on the Exodus*, II, 62, 68.
8. *Demonstration*, 10.
9. A notable example is the icon of the Trinity painted by the Russian monk Andrei Rublev in 1425. This, now in the Tretiakov Gallery in Moscow, was declared by a Council in the sixteenth century to be the model for all icons of the Trinity. The three figures are virtually identical young men, with wings and haloes. Only their dress is

the word *angel* in this context would be assumed to be heretical. Why this should be so is something of a mystery. It is tempting to speculate that, in the fourth-century battle for the Divinity of the Son, the word *angel* too easily suggested a *creature*, and so was abandoned by the orthodox. But there is no evidence of this. 'Angel' was not an Arian term, and Athanasius himself is aware that, as a description of function, it can be applied to the Son.[10]

The language of translation may have played a large part in the matter. Whereas in Greek *angelos* continued to be used in the functional sense, Latin versions of scripture rendered it by *nuntius* when it referred to a human being; otherwise they transliterated it as *angelus*. This may explain why it is unusual in the west to use *angel* of a human being. It does not quite explain why it ceased to be used of divine persons. But it did so cease. For centuries it has been an unchallenged premiss that 'angel' describes the nature of non-human created beings.

Two particular writings may have helped to ensure this. The first is the *Epistle to the Hebrews*. Chapters 1 and 2 of this deal with the Incarnate Son's superiority to 'angels', a point illustrated by seven quotations from the O.T. and vigorous argument. This Epistle was one whose canonical authority was considerably disputed in the early church. But its general acceptance in the fourth century must have

---

varied. There is an interesting difference of opinion among Orthodox commentators about the identity of the separate persons. The central figure, whose clothes are in the boldest colours, might obviously seem to be God the Father, and so most commentators think. But there is much to be said for the minority view that, with his greater 'concreteness' and his deacon's stole, he is the Son. But the identity of the separate persons may not have been the iconographer's main concern. He is depicting scripture and the liturgy: 'Blessed Abraham, you saw them, and received the Godhead, both one and three.'

10. Commenting on Genesis 48.15,16, he says, '(Jacob) showed that it was no created angel but the Word of God whom he joined to the Father in his prayer... For knowing that he is also called the Father's "Angel of mighty counsel", he said that none other than he was the giver of blessing and deliverer from evil.' *Oratio Contra Arianos*, III, xii.

made it difficult to retain the less limited meaning of 'angel'. The second, and this had an enormous influence, was the Pseudo-Dionysius, an unknown Syrian of the sixth century writing under the name of St Paul's Athenian convert. He gave full formulation to the doctrine of the nine orders of angelic beings (familiar to modern worshippers through Athelstan Riley's hymn, 'Ye watchers and ye holy ones', English Hymnal 519). The teaching of his *Celestial Hierarchies* is summed up thus: 'God encounters Man only through a "mean"... He cannot deny that Theophanies, direct appearances of God Himself to patriarchs and prophets, *seem* to occur in the Old Testament. But he is quite sure that this never really happens. These visions were in reality mediated through celestial, but created, beings.'[11]

It is surprising that the misunderstanding is not more widely challenged today, especially now that the influence of the Pseudo-Dionysius has waned. The idea that the Nicene doctrine of the Trinity is a Hellenistic philosophical construction imposed on an original simple gospel is nonsense. What you find as you go back is not simplicity but complexity of a different sort; and it does not seem that we have properly evaluated that earlier complexity.[12]

The doctrine of the Trinity therefore, at least in the west, has been cut off from its biblical and primitive basis by the false premiss that the word *angel* means, invariably, a created being. It has had to find other terminology, some of which is abstract, some misleading. It may be too late to revive angelic trinitarianism, even though classical angelology is, in modern western Christianity, even more dead than the doctrine of the Trinity.[13] At least this particular discarded image ought continually to recall us to the foundation of the doctrine, namely, the Angel of the Presence in the Old Testament.

11. C.S. Lewis, *The Discarded Image*, CUP, 1964, pp.72-73.
12. In this matter there is often little to choose between 'orthodox' and 'radical' scholars. To take an example of each: B. Lonergan in *The Way to Nicea*, Darton, Longman and Todd, E.T. 1976, summarizes angelic trinitarianism with clinical efficiency, but sees it only as a false development. D. Cupitt in *The Debate about Christ*, SCM,

1979, dismisses angelology as 'fanciful and eccentric speculations' (p.126), though this seriously compromises his claim that Judaism was 'a pure and rational prophetic monotheism' from which historic Christianity is a regrettable declension. James D.G. Dunn, *Christology in the Making*, SCM, 1980, has little difficulty in demonstrating that the New Testament does not use 'angel' language of Jesus. Curiously, however, he takes the fact that *'the "angel of Yahweh" is simply a way of speaking about Yahweh himself'* (p.150, his italics) as a criticism of the Fathers' usage, when it is in fact the justification of it. See further, chapter 5.

13. The question should at least be asked whether the angel or angels at the Nativity and Resurrection of Our Lord are not to be understood like the Old Testament's angel of Yahweh—that is, God himself, announcing the great events of salvation. It will be noticed how rarely 'angels' and the incarnate Son appear together at the same time and place. The rare exceptions appear to be after the Temptation in the wilderness (Mark 1:13) and St Luke's Agony (Luke 22:43).

CHAPTER THREE

Father and Son

Although God calls Israel as a whole, and its king, his Son,
men in the Old Testament rarely call God 'Father'. As a
biblical title, 'Son of God' does not necessarily imply
divinity, as it did in the polytheistic pagan world. When,
therefore, Jesus is designated 'Son of God' it cannot be
assumed that this is a title of deity. It may mean he is the
true Israel, or it may be messianic, the style of the king.

Jesus, however, calls God 'Father' with an intensity and
frequency which was unique. This usage is one of the dom-
inating features of St. John's gospel, but it is not found
there only. The typical language of St. John appears in
Matthew 11:25-27 (= Luke 10:21,22), the 'Johannine
thunderbolt in the Synoptic sky', and indeed permeates the
New Testament.

God does nothing suddenly and Jesus disclaimed origi-
nality. It is unsatisfactory therefore to treat his awareness
of God's fatherhood as revelation without precedent. It is
likely to have some background and 'human' origin. But
what? God's description as, or invocation as, 'Father' in
the Old Testament is much less frequent than is commonly
supposed. It is found mainly in the psalms and the later

Isaiah. There is nothing standard or taken-for-granted
about it. Indeed, the usage, when it appears, seems consciously 'poetic' and metaphorical. God is 'Father of the
fatherless' (Psalms 68:5). It is '*As a father* pities his
children, so the Lord pities those who fear him' (Psalm
103:13). 'Thou art our Father, though Abraham does not
know us and Israel does not acknowledge us' (Isaiah
63:16). The clearest confession, 'O Lord thou art our
Father' (Isaiah 64:8), is at once qualified by a different
analogy: 'We are the clay and thou art our potter.' (Cf.
Malachi 2:10, 'Have we not all one Father? Has not one
God created us?') Particularly significant is the prophecy
about the Son of David: ' "He shall cry to me, Thou art my
Father" ' (Psalm 89:26). This might well be the starting point
of Jesus's usage. But the royal and messianic style about
which he was, to say the least, cautious, can hardly bear
the weight of the frequency, authority and confidence with
which he calls God 'my Father'. Even the Israel-Son,
responding to the loving Father of Hosea's moving words,
(Hosea 11:1-4; cf. Jeremiah 31:9) does not seem to provide
the range and intimacy which the language of the New
Testament requires.

It has been suggested[1] that in this language there is a
concealed parable of human family relationships. 'The Son
can do nothing by himself; he does only what he sees the
Father doing' (John 5:19). This could equally well be translated, 'A son can do nothing by himself; he does only what
he sees his father doing." This suggestion commends itself
to scholars who wish to 'reduce' the Father-Son language
from terms of divine status to those of the human family.

But the idea is profound and far-reaching. It suggests
that the characteristic language and outlook of Jesus is
based less on the formal title 'Son of God', with all its
ambiguities, and more on the analogy of the human
family. 'A son honours his father... If then I am a father,
where is my honour?' (Malachi 1:6). For Jesus the human

1. e.g. by C.H. Dodd, *More New Testament Studies*, Manchester UP,
    1968, pp.30-40; J.A.T. Robinson, *The Human Face of God*, SCM,
    1972, pp.186-188.

family would be found primarily in the stories of the Old Testament, which contains several outstanding examples of father-son relationships, by no means all ideal. This, indeed, rather than marriage, is the dominant human tie in the Old Testament, which F.D. Maurice might have called a book about fathers and sons.

In most cases the relationship is described from the father's viewpoint. Isaac, for example, is the beloved, or only, son of Abraham and Sarah, born as a result of divine promise in their old age. When God commands him to be sacrificed, Abraham's anguish is not only one of human affection, but for the divine promise to his posterity. Joseph and Benjamin are not the only sons of Jacob; but they are the sons of his old age by his beloved wife Rachel, and the whole elaborate story turns on that special relationship. Absalom is not the only son of David, but he was uniquely beloved and uniquely treacherous. 'O Absalom, my son...' Two other prominent Old Testament sons are Jacob, who at his mother's behest plays a dirty trick on his dying father Isaac, and Jonathan, often forced to choose between loyalty to his father Saul and his friendship with David.

If then we ask whence, humanly speaking, did Jesus derive his sense of sonship, is not the answer, from these stories, heard in the synagogue and making a powerful appeal to one who was himself to become a great storyteller? He is, to his heavenly Father, the Son those other sons were, *or ought to have been*, to their human fathers. He is the Isaac who would indeed be sacrificed and has not, this time, been kept in the dark about his Father's purpose. He is the Jacob who needed no deceit to be the true Israel, the Joseph who went out from his Father to do great things without having nearly destroyed himself by his youthful pride. He is an articulate Benjamin, responding, as the original Benjamin never does, in word and deed to his Father's love. He is a Jonathan who does not have to choose between his Father and his friends. He is a faithful Absalom, dying for his Father's kingdom and not in rebellion against it.

This claim or standpoint, that Jesus is to his heavenly

Father as the sons of the patriarchs were, or should have been, to their fathers, may underlie a number of New Testament passages, especially some that usually seem obscure or enigmatic. What it means to be a son of Abraham is a common question, but most frequently refers not to the unique Sonship of Jesus, but to the quality of his Jewish contemporaries. As such it is raised by the Baptist and is the theme of the Tabernacles controversy. But, 'Your father Abraham rejoiced to see my day' (John 8:56), suggests that what Abraham saw was the true Isaac. The comparison of Jesus with Jacob is required by the Israel-theme and by the choice of the Twelve. Comparison between Jesus and Joseph is less prominent than one might expect, but there may be a hint of it in John 4, where in preparation for the conversation with the Samaritan woman the evangelist comments that they were 'near to the parcel of ground that Jacob gave to his son Joseph' (4:5).

'Son of David', by contrast, is a prominent title in the New Testament and one about which Jesus was cautious, no doubt because, like Messiah, it had a conventional and popular meaning which he did not accept. His typical wish that his contemporaries should see through the usual meaning of a title to the truth within or below is indicated in Mark 12:35 and parallels: 'How say the scribes that the Christ is the Son of David? David himself calls him Lord, and whence is he his Son?' But evidently Jesus did not wish to abandon the Davidic theme altogether—witness the appeal to David's example in the Sabbath controversy (Mark 2:25ff) and the claim that 'a greater than Solomon is here' (Matthew 12:42).

So if the style 'Son of God' bears only ambiguous witness to the divinity of Jesus, the analogy of the human father and son is stronger and clearer. A father has primacy and seniority, but father and son are 'of the same substance', and the human analogy leads to the Nicene creed, with the famous expression by which the church sought to safeguard the full divinity of the Son. The 'Liberal Protestantism' of the late nineteenth and early twentieth centuries found the central New Testament message in the Fatherhood of God, with which was linked the brotherhood of man. But the central New Testament doctrine is the Sonship of Jesus, without which the Fatherhood of God is completely misunderstood.

It is at this point that we may expect the analogy to shed some light on what usually appears as very puzzling in trinitarian language and thought. The creed describes Jesus the Son as 'eternally begotten of the Father' (the older translation was 'begotten of his Father before all worlds'). The idea was first given full expression by Origen (c.185-254). Arius, the arch-heretic of the fourth century, agreed that the Son existed before time was created, but nevertheless thought the Son originated at what was, in effect, a point in time, for he claimed that 'there was when he was not': hence he was not truly God. Athanasius and subsequent orthodoxy denied this, not always very convincingly. For, in the analogy of a father and son, the father exists before the son, and 'there is (a time) when the son is not'.

So in a sense the great fourth-century controversy was a controversy about how to apply the father-son analogy. Arius said, in effect, it is about *origins*. The Father is superior to the Son in that he exists before him and can do without him. There is enough commonsense about that to commend it, both in the fourth century and later. But the orthodox replied, not always very clearly, that the analogy is about the *relationship* of father and grown-up son. The Old Testament stories are all about such a relationship. Where they are concerned with the details of birth (as with Isaac) this tells us nothing about the generation of the Eternal Son, who is 'co-eternal' with his Father. And if the Son is in any way 'subordinate' to the Father, this subordination is not because he is subsequent, or could in principle be dispensed with, even less that he is not really God. Subordination, if it is at all an appropriate term, can be understood only within the setting of the relationship of father and son and the unity which embraces them.

For the analogy which safeguards the Godhead of Jesus also looks like encouraging a pluralistic doctrine of the Trinity. 'Father' and 'Son' are two people. Are we not in danger of making the price of the Son's divinity an abandonment of the One God, as critics of the doctrine of the Trinity have often maintained?

This, however, is to project on to the biblical literature a sense of personal individuality which, though found in Ezekiel 18, by no means holds the field alone. The fact that Israel as a community is described as God's Son should warn us that in the Bible individual people do not have the hard modern edges we are accustomed to. Like us they have physical bodies, which are the basis of individuality; but they are less inclined than we are to equate personal identity with the individual and more inclined to find it in a 'corporate personality', of which marriage is the obvious example. This is the purport of the 'one flesh' of Genesis 2:24, and the exposition of marriage in the Epistle to the Ephesians ought to bring home to us how much biblical and modern categories differ. 'He that loves his own wife loves himself.' The fraternal relationship of Moses and Aaron is another example. Yahweh says to Moses, 'You shall speak to him and put the words in his mouth... he will be the mouthpiece, and you will be the god he speaks for' (Exodus 4:15,16).

Although modern psychological theory tends to be individualistic, much modern practice is not individualistic at all. The modern person who wants to 'be himself' or 'find himself' often does so in a highly corporate, not to say tribal, unit—the football crowd, the street gang, the social or vocational unit, the political movement. The 'corporate personality' is, in various guises, as familiar to us as it was to ancient Israel.

The father-son relationship on which Jesus drew is a corporate personality in which the son will perform and execute what the father has in mind. If Isaac dies, Abraham's life will be a living death, for God's promise on which his life was founded will be contradicted. If Jacob loses Benjamin, he will himself die, say the brothers, for his life is bound up in the lad's life. David, 'bound in the bundle of the living' with his beloved son Absalom, must see the unity of the royal house and of Israel shattered.

In the presence of their fathers the sons have no independent personalities. Isaac asks only leading questions. Benjamin is silent. Joseph, torn away from his father, partly through his own fault, must act independently.

With his father restored to him, he resumes filial dependence, at least in family matters, and his brothers fear, unnecessarily, that his character will change after Jacob's death. Jonathan's independence is the corollary of Saul's collapse, and Absalom asserts his independence only by a rebellion which destroys him and desolates his father. When the young David came to Saul's notice because of his victory over Goliath, Saul's sole interest appears to be to discover the name of the boy's father (1 Samuel 17:55-58). Having failed to find out from anyone else, Saul was reduced, by necessity or curiosity, to asking David himself. 'Whose son are you, young man?' And David answered, 'I am the son of your servant Jesse the Bethlehemite.' Both Saul and David assumed that David's identity resided in his father. The Edwardian matron, asking about the unknown debutante, 'Who is she?' meant, 'Who is her father?'.

Much of what Jesus says in St. John's gospel about his relation to his Father goes far beyond any modern analogy of the human family, and as a sudden revelation of the inner life of the Trinity it seems to many modern critics incredible on the lips of the historical Jesus. But if Jesus took those earlier fathers and sons as the starting-point of his thought, it is not incredible at all. Like the Old Testament sons, he has no independent personality. Everything he says to and of his Father is a confession of their unity-in-distinction. Like Joseph, he must do and suffer many things in a strange land. And like Joseph he is articulate about his yearning for his Father and his Father's house, where his inmost being remains.[2]

---

2. A.M. Farrer, in *A Study in St. Mark* (Dacre, 1951), suggested that the much-discussed title *Son of Man* might mean, on the lips of Jesus, Son of Adam, rather than be derived from apocalyptic or apocryphal speculation. ' "The Son of Man" was not, and never had been, the name for a mysterious allegorical figure destined to fly down from the sky in the last days' (p.285). Cf. J.D.G. Dunn, op.cit., 'The thought of the Son of Man as a pre-existent heavenly figure does not seem to have emerged in Jewish or Christian circles before the last decades of the first century A.D.' Since Adam = Man, the title might be virtually equivalent to *the Son* used absolutely; or it might associate Jesus with Abel.

CHAPTER FOUR

Purpose and Memory

Parts of the biblical narrative have a leisurely character
with a good deal of repetition which the modern reader
finds tedious. Two examples may serve. In the story of the
betrothal of Isaac (which is vital if he is to fulfil his role as
Abraham's son) the family's servant foresees, in prayer,
the encounter with the right girl (Genesis 24:10-14). The
meeting then takes place as foreseen (24:15-20) and both
forecast and event are then recalled (24:34-50). In the Acts
of the Apostles the crucial movement of the Church to the
gentiles is elaborately dealt with. First, Cornelius is prepared (Acts 10:1-8), then Peter is prepared by a three-fold
vision (10:9-16) and informed of Cornelius's preparation
(10:30-33). Secondly, Peter preaches to the gentiles, the
Spirit is given to them and they are baptized (10:34-45).
Thirdly, in answer to critics, Peter recalls his own and
Cornelius's preparation, and the event (11:1-18).

Repetition serves to emphasize the importance of an
incident, and its particular form will, says the critic, be
determined by the writer or final editor. But the faith and
outlook of a writer (or editor) is an essential part of

scripture, and evidently in these cases repetition is neither haphazard nor uncontrolled. It has a distinct threefold pattern—the three elements being first, counsel, plan or purpose, manifesting itself in some form of prediction; second, act or event, and third, remembrance, especially of the unity of plan and event. It is the threefold structure which brings conviction that the action is God's, and initiates thankful response. Rebecca's family said, 'This is from the Lord' (Genesis 24:50). Peter's critics said, 'This means that God has granted life-giving repentance to the gentiles also' (Acts 11:18).

This threefold structure of action is very widespread, and perhaps present to some degree in every biblical happening. But it is not always as explicit and complete as in the two cases quoted. The central event of the New Testament, the death and resurrection of Jesus, is foretold (three times in Mark, 8:31; 9:31,32; 10:32-34) and the identity of plan and event is central to Peter's Pentecostal sermon (Acts 2:22-24).

It is not difficult to see that, in ordinary human affairs, effective action requires plan and preparation which make possible, and indeed require, an element of prediction. The brain-wave can be a curse. If acted on, it can produce quite unforeseen and disastrous results. Intricate action, like that of a military operation, must be planned in detail, and, to be effective, it must in a sense already have 'happened' in mind and imagination. Far-reaching changes in society and politics must be 'thought' before they can be brought about. In fact they are often 'thought' long before—a phenomenon observed and famously described by Oscar Wilde as 'nature imitating art'. Likewise, the power and importance of memory is that it enables individuals and societies to achieve unity and coherence and to relate one experience rationally to another.

But what appears haltingly and imperfectly in man and man's action is the essential character of God and God's action. 'Before they came to pass I announced them to you' (Isaiah 48:5). 'Now I have told you before it takes place, so that when it does take place you may believe' (John 14:29).

Purposeful divine action—divine action is, by definition,

purposeful—requires plan and preparation, which is the source, fount and origin of action. God as this source is what Christian theology calls the Father, and from him all else, both divine and created, comes. But God is not knowable until he acts, and he acts as Son, who executes the plan and will of the Father. Even then the fulness of action is not complete until the unity of plan and act has been perceived in recollection. Maybe the process, in human minds, makes the forecast more explicit than it might otherwise have been, but even this human foible serves to show the, power of the threefold pattern. It is as Spirit that God remembers and causes men to remember.

From the triune pattern of action we might call God Planner, Doer and Remembrancer; but they are poor, thin words (except perhaps the third) compared with Father, Son and Spirit, to which they nevertheless form a genuine parallel. Each is fully God, none is complete without the others and there is no fourth term.

Extended on to a large enough scale, this pattern of activity might be said to merge into the very being of God. At the centre of the panorama is the act of God, the Son, the Incarnate, the Dying-and-Rising One. What goes before is prophetic witness, the plan of the Father receiving preliminary and varied expression. What comes after is the Spirit's remembrance, the life of the Church, including the writing of the New Testament and its conviction of the unity of the act with its varied preliminaries. The pattern of the divine being is also, on the appropriate scale, the pattern of man made in God's image; and the pattern of divine activity is also the pattern of effective human activity.

Some caution is necessary. The threshold pattern may be taken as an echo of the threefold being of God. It does not mean that each divine person performs his own business in isolation from the others—any more than another echo, creation, redemption and sanctification, can be parcelled out among the persons. External works of God are always works of the three persons in unity, even while those external works disclose something of the pattern of the divine being.

The plan or purpose of the Father receiving preliminary expression might be called prophecy, and there is much, in both testaments, to associate the Spirit with prophecy. Does not this overturn the pattern outlined above? It needs to be remembered that *Spirit* in the Old Testament by no means always means the third term of the Trinity. As will be argued later, this more precise meaning is due to Jesus's own usage. Moreover, though 'prophecy' in the New Testament still contains an element of prediction, it is prediction based on remembrance, as the Christ who has come indicates the lineaments of 'the Christ that is to be'. Paul's 'prediction' of the general resurrection in 1 Corinthians 15 is based on his remembrance of Christ's resurrection. The Apocalypse sums it up: 'The testimony of Jesus is the spirit of prophecy' (Revelation 19:10).

One of the last things that C.S. Lewis wrote is a moving and impressive interpretation of resurrection in terms of memory.[1]

> We already have some feeble and intermittent power
> of raising dead sensations from their graves. I mean,
> of course, memory . . . I mean . . . that memory as
> we now know it is a dim foretaste, a mirage even, of
> a power which the soul, or rather Christ in the soul

1. Sayers had anticipated him in one of those pregnant but almost throw-away passages with which her writing abounds. Speaking, in the course of developing her analogy of the Trinity, of the writing of a book and the vulnerability of a book once written to censorship or other hazards, she says, 'We must, however, be careful to see that nobody reads it before we take steps to eliminate it, otherwise it may disconcert us by rising again—either as a new Idea in somebody's mind, or even (if somebody has a good memory) in a resurrected body, substantially the same though made of new materials. In this respect, Herod showed himself much more competent and realistic than Pilate or Caiaphas. He grasped the principle that if you are to destroy the Word, you must do so before it has time to communicate itself. Crucifixion gets there too late' (*The Mind of the Maker*, p.91). At the mention of a 'good memory' Sayers may have had in the back of her mind the famous incident in 1835 when Thomas Carlyle's manuscript of *The French Revolution* was used by Mill's housemaid to light the fire. Carlyle recreated the work by a prodigious act of memory.

. . . will exercise hereafter. It need no longer be inter-
mittent. Above all, it need no longer be private to the
soul in which it occurs . . . We tend to think of the
soul as somehow 'inside' the body. But the glorified
body of the resurrection as I conceive it—the sen-
suous life raised from its death—will be inside the
soul. As God is not in space but space is in God.[2]

Lewis has no directly trinitarian intention when he writes
these words. But 'Christ in the soul' is, exactly, the Holy
Spirit. The Holy Spirit will recreate within us the sensa-
tions derived from matter and bring them to an intensity of
which our present life is only a foretaste. 'Memory' as we
now know it is a clue to this mystery.

It may be the clue to another mystery also. The Church
celebrates the Eucharist in obedience to Christ's command,
'Do this in remembrance of me'. But emphasis on remem-
brance has been thought to imply a 'low' view of the
Eucharist, the *'nuda commemoratio'* which the Council of
Trent attributed to Protestants[3] and which the English
Archbishops disclaimed in their *Responsio* to Leo XIII in
1897.[4]

In attempting to make the Eucharist more than this, the
Council said that in it Christ was indeed offered again, but
'in a different mode' and 'without blood'. The rational
nature of such an offering the Council was not able to
explain. Meanwhile, Protestants said that since there was
no repetition of Christ's death there could be no repetition
of his sacrifice.

But if it is true that memory, remembrance, is the necessary third dimension of the divine pattern, there is a way
through this sacramental Scylla and Charybdis. It is a
necessary part of the pattern, not an addition to it or an
optional extra; for until preparation and event are remembered they are not fruitful or complete. A genuine
remembrance of the all-sufficient sacrifice cannot be 'bare';

2. *Letters to Malcolm Chiefly on Prayer*, Bles, 1963, p.155-156.
3. Session XXII, Canon 3, Sept. 1562.
4. *Anglican Orders*, SPCK, 1932, p.35.

it must issue in the oblation of ourselves, our souls and bodies as one body in Christ. If there is such a thing as the memory of some past act now totally without significance, that remembrance would be 'bare'. But the remembrance of any significant act is part of the nature and fulness of the act itself.

The eucharistic pattern then is of prediction (proximately, the Last Supper), event (the Cross) and remembrance (the Eucharist). The unity which binds the three is the Son's self-oblation to the Father, present in the supper, consummated in his own blood, and effective in the many who are made one body with him in the Eucharist. The distinction of prediction, event and remembrance is in no way annulled by their unity.[5]

We recall the long tradition of a special relationship between the Holy Spirit and the Eucharist—a relationship not easy to define or express, for the Spirit is self-effacing and (unlike some of his would-be special disciples) does not draw attention to himself. But if the Spirit is, essentially, the Remembrancer, his relation to the Eucharist is fundamental and not dependent on explicit liturgical reference to him, however desirable such reference may be.

5. 'The ... Sacrament ... may be illustrated from the composition and
    playing of music; there is first the music in the composer's mind,
    second there is the music actualized in sound, third there is the
    musical score whereby the music may be realised for each
    generation afresh throughout all time.... We may conceive God's
    divine purpose of redemption, the co-eternal Word, as
    corresponding with the music in the composer's mind; the Word
    made flesh corresponds with the music uttered by the musician; the
    Sacrament answers to the readings of the score whereby for all time
    the wonder is extended and renewed.' N. Micklem, *Christian
    Worship*, OUP, 1933. Though not put forward as an analogy of the
    Trinity, this corresponds closely with the analogy described in
    Chapter 9.

CHAPTER FIVE

The Word and the Words

Word, Name, Wisdom and Spirit are all prominent in describing the being and activity of God in the Bible, and in both testaments. There is much controversy as to how, and to what extent, they are distinct from God-in-himself, or, in other words and in technical trinitarian language, whether they constitute separate 'persons'.

In their Old Testament origin these four important terms all depend on analogy; that is, what is observed to be true of man is also true (on a different scale) of God, and vice versa. God is, at various times, credited with most of the physical organs of man—G.A.F. Knight gives a convenient list in his *Christian Theology of the Old Testament*.[1] This physical correspondence may well have been regarded from early days as symbolic for a God who was, to the ordinary human eye, invisible; for if God is to be pictured at all, he must be pictured as a human being, even though Ezekiel, with startling modernity, made the attempt to picture him as a machine (Ezekiel 1) [2].

1. SCM 2nd Edition 1964, Chapter 5.
2. Cf. C.S. Lewis, *Miracles*, Bles 1947, p.139.

But for the structure of being, especially being-in-activity, there must be some correspondence between God and man, and the whole biblical revelation assumes that there is. Did not God make man 'in his own image' (Genesis 1:26-28)? This itself rules out the idolatry of 'birds and beasts and creeping things', while other aspects of the revelation preclude a variety of gods and goddesses whose morals are all-too-human.

Men express themselves, and communicate, by word and speech. So therefore does God. Man's word can have a distinct existence. Amos's words, once uttered (Amos 7:10), constituted a sort of physical threat to Jeroboam and Israel. Samuel's words achieved results (1 Samuel 3:19; 4:1). Man's word, though not conceivably separate from his being, is nevertheless distinct, his being-in-activity, his *alter ego*.

God's Word, therefore, is not a strange or far-fetched concept. It is essentially analogical. But it is extensively developed, especially in the Psalms and the Wisdom literature. Because God is a rational God who communicates with man through law and prophecy and writings, his Word becomes his essential instrument. It may be that it replaces the angel of the presence (Chapter 2) when 'angel' had come to mean usually a created being.

The *Name* of God, and the names of his creatures, occupy a prominent place all through the Bible. The Name is a revelation of identity, an admission to communion. In the Garden of Eden Adam *names* the animals, establishing their nature and his relation to them (Genesis 2:19,20). The name is a distinct entity, with a definite meaning; but it is intended to correspond to the reality of the person. 'Proper names in the early period were evidently given to represent an idea that the parents' hopes would be embodied in their children.'[3] A change of role or status might divide a person from his name, and necessitate a new name—a common happening in the Bible. So Abram changed his name to Abraham (Genesis 17:5) and Jacob to Israel (Genesis 32:28; 35:10). Naomi, on her return to Bethlehem, said to the

3. G.A.F. Knight, op.cit., p.41.

women, 'Do not call me Naomi (Pleasant), call me Mara (Bitter), for the Almighty has dealt very bitterly with me' (Ruth 1:20); a change of name which was happily not permanent.

If men have a name, so has God (Chapter 2, note 1), and angelic manifestation puts it within reach of man. Jacob, having himself been renamed by the 'man' he wrestled with, said, 'Tell me, I pray, your name.' But he said, 'Why is it that you ask my name?' (Genesis 32:29). The Name is revealed to Moses by the Angel at the bush (Exodus 3:13-15), and when it came to be considered too sacred to be pronounced it was represented by the Hebrew and Greek titles translated as LORD. So 'Jesus is Lord' (Romans 10:9; 1 Corinthians 12:3) means that the divine name is his name. The 'name of Jesus' (Philippians 2:10) is not 'Jesus' but LORD, and baptism 'in the name of Jesus Christ' (Acts 2:38) is the same as baptism 'in the name of the Father and of the Son and of the Holy Spirit' (Matthew 28:19) because it is one and the same name, LORD, the personal name of God.

Spirit (which means 'wind' or 'breath') often seems a word which emphasizes the difference between God and man. The Egyptians are men, and not God; and their horses are flesh, not spirit' (Isaiah 31:3). The parallelism here suggests that man is flesh, limited, vulnerable; God is spirit, elusive, powerful. 'God is spirit' (John 4:24) as distinct from those whose worship is geographically limited to Jerusalem or Mount Gerizim.

But 'spirit' is used analogically, as St. Paul explicitly says: 'Who knows what a man is, but the man's own spirit within him? *In the same way*, only the Spirit knows what God is' (1 Corinthians 2:11). When Elisha successfully parted the waters of the Jordan, the sons of the prophets cried, 'The spirit of Elijah has settled on Elisha' (2 Kings 2:15).

Though, therefore, man is not 'spirit' as such, he *has* spirit, or a spirit. He can transcend himself, and like the wind, itself invisible, can have visible effect. In the thought of St. Paul and St. John, following, no doubt, the teaching of Jesus, the word 'spirit' is becoming more markedly analogical, without entirely losing its elusive character.

Wisdom is rather like *Spirit*, with the emphasis on the rational. It must be expressed in words (did not Solomon utter three thousand proverbs, and his songs number one thousand and five?—1 Kings 4:32). But it precedes the word as an inner disposition (or, in the case of man, a gift of God) and it also has external effect.[4]

Word, Name, Wisdom and Spirit, therefore, in biblical thought never leave the essential context of the analogy between God and man. The structure of both the divine and the human being is already becoming apparent in the Old Testament. But terminology is still fluid, and it is a mistake to interpret Old Testament terms solely in a later trinitarian sense. 'Word' is perhaps well established for being-in-expression, and is to be given Christological prominence by St. John. 'In the beginning was the Word ... and the Word was made flesh' (John 1:1 and 1:14). Even so, Word is not destined to become the main term for being-in-expression. It is not surprising that being-in-expression should be the first trinitarian mode to acquire a definable technical term, for it is being-in-expression alone that is accessible to other beings. The discovery, however inevitable and essential, that being-in-expression is the second mode in a trinity, requires a degree of experience and self-awareness not quickly developed. It was not apparent before the New Testament that, as a trinitarian term, Wisdom would drop out[5] and Spirit become established for the third mode. The choice of the three terms

4. This passage was written before the appearance of James D.G. Dunn's magisterial work, *Christology in the Making*, SCM 1980. Dunn concludes that there were no personifications or entities distinct from Yahweh of which Jesus could be regarded as the incarnation. The ... intermediary figures ... Spirit, Wisdom, Word, are *im*properly so called, since they never really reach the status of divine beings independent of God.... They all remain ... ways of speaking of God's powerful interaction with the world and his people.... Their pre-existence is the pre-existence of God (pp.252-53).' This conclusion, that Christ is not to be explained as the manifestation of some pre-existent intermediary being, is vital for trinitarian theology.

5. Dunn (op.cit.) holds that of these three terms, it was Wisdom

Father, Son and Spirit must be regarded as due to the teaching of Jesus himself[6] and the selection he made from the rich and varied material of the Old Testament. One might deduce the trinitarian nature of God from the Old Testament, but one could not deduce the Christian terminology.

---

which first formed the basis of the doctrine of the incarnation. 'In using Wisdom language of Christ ... Paul ... understood the Christ-event as God's own action on behalf of men (p.255).' Having performed this vital function, Wisdom may have dropped into the background because it was not the main term favoured by Jesus. It never established itself as the term of one specific trinitarian mode.

6. Cf. 'Go therefore and make disciples of all nations, baptizing them in the name of the Father and of the Son and of the Holy Spirit' (Matthew 28:19). Radicals and sceptics will do anything to discredit the terminology of the glorified Christ's commission, but it is textually unassailable. It may be regarded as the briefest possible summary of the teaching found *in extenso* in St. John, and as true to the mind and language of Jesus as anything in the four gospels.

CHAPTER SIX

Person and Personality

The modern world may be unsure of God, but it is confident that it knows all about persons. Persons, it would hold, are individual, self-conscious, rational beings. Three persons would constitute a family or a body corporate which might live in harmony and act in unity. But that harmony and unity is dependent on, and at the mercy of, independent minds and wills. Therefore, to call God three persons is either meaningless, or it makes God a family; an idea some modern theologians have found acceptable.

In technical language the Latin word *persona* has been used from the third century, as the equivalent of the Greek *hypostasis*, to describe that of which the Godhead is, or has, three. But when used by the Fathers it did not necessarily mean what it means now. It is not easy to say what it *did* mean. Simply by derivation, *persona* means the mask which the classical actor wore, and hence the role that he played. Christian theology was quick to point out that Father, Son and Spirit are not roles played by God as an actor might in his time play 'many parts'.[1] The adoption of

See Introduction, p.10 and note 2.

disguises, often for immoral purposes, was common for pagan gods, but not for the God of the Bible. The three 'persons' of God are structural. They are true of God in his essential being, and they are exhaustive; there is no fourth or subsequent person.

A 'low' meaning of person as 'mask' or 'role' continued in theological use long after the days of the Fathers. So Luther can say, 'For person is properly speaking only face or countenance or mask (*larva*) ... and it is that quality or quantity by which a man may be considered from without; and the meaning of "God is no respecter of persons" is that he does not regard who, what kind, how much. What then does he regard? The answer is: the heart.'[2]

It seems, however, that not long after the word *persona* had been adopted for trinitarian use, it acquired a common meaning which rendered it increasingly unsuitable for such use. If the argument of earlier chapters is valid, in biblical thought two or more individual beings, persons in the old sense, might constitute one personality, one person in the newer sense. This would be true of the great father-son relationships of the Old Testament. It is true of the marriage relationship. 'One flesh' is very close to 'one personality', and St. Paul is very explicit: 'He who loves his wife loves himself. For no man ever hates his own flesh, but nourishes and cherishes it' (Ephesians 5:28,29). But, spurred on by the Holy Spirit in the Church, the individual is on the upgrade. The person is becoming, and the word is coming to mean, personality—the self-conscious being projecting his own image, experiencing its result, and so complete in himself. It is difficult to date 'the discovery of the individual'.[3] The process goes on unevenly over centuries. Spengler pointed out the significant difference between pre-Christian and post-Christian language. 'Instead of *sum*, Gothic *im*, we say *ich bin*, I am, *je suis*.'[4]

---

2. *Galatians*, 1517.
3. Colin Morris's book with this title (SPCK 1972) ascribes it to the years 1050-1200.
4. Quoted by W.P. Witcutt, *The Rise and Fall of the Individual*, SPCK 1958.

Now, to make sense, a separate pronoun must be used, whereas previously the form of the verb expressed, as a subsidiary meaning, the 'person'. Post-Christian usage suggests the action of self-motivated wills and an increased sense of individuality. St. Augustine of Hippo, as is well known, doubted whether 'persona' was the right word to describe Father, Son and Spirit,[5] and well he might; for Augustine was the first man sufficiently self-conscious to write an autobiography (the *Confessions*), and in his theology he continually sought an analogy of the Trinity in the individual human soul. Though he did not find an analogy which fully satisfied him, he never lost confidence that he was looking in the right place. The greatest trinitarian theologian of the twentieth century, Karl Barth, shares and extends Augustine's doubts about the suitability of the word 'person' for its traditional and technical use.[6]

There is therefore a strong element of paradox in the terminology frozen in the Church's formularies. Two (or more) human persons might constitute an appropriate analogy of the Trinity in the days before 'the discovery of the individual'. But as the concept of individual personality fills out, a plurality of human persons becomes increasingly inappropriate as a guide to the divine Persons, and instead the single human personality becomes the essential analogue. Why this change in, and extension of, human personality should have occurred is one of the most profound historical questions which can be asked, and the answers cannot be discussed or evaluated here. But the writer's conviction is that it is that unique relationship with the triune God in Christianity which has filled out and extended the individual human being until he has grown

---

5. *De Trinitate*, V 9, VII 4.
6. *The Doctrine of the Word of God*, Clark, E.T. 1936, pp.407-414. Failure to take seriously the term *person* and its difficulties is one of the limitations of that pugnacious piece of orthodoxy, E.L. Mascall's *Whatever happened to the Human Mind?* SPCK 1980. Thus K. Rahner 'makes unnecessarily heavy weather with the term "person" (p.167 note 13). Unless with Rahner (to say nothing of Augustine and Barth) we wrestle with such terms we shall not commend the doctrine.

up into the image of the Trinity. The impact of Christianity has been such as to render its own terminology obsolete. That may be inconvenient or annoying. But the development is in no sense a 'failure' of Christianity; quite the reverse. Even the teasing question of terminology is quite explicable once some presuppositions have been questioned.

CHAPTER SEVEN

The Search for Analogy

Linguistic usage and other factors deprived the doctrine of
the Trinity of the 'angel' as its biblical and imaginative
basis. It used instead a number of terms already current in
the Mediterranean world of the early Christian centuries —
in Greek, *ousia* and *hypostasis*, in Latin *substantia* and
persona. When used in trinitarian theology these words
acquire a technical sense. But 'in the world' they were not
technical but varied a great deal according to the context.
Ousia, for example, could mean 'being' as distinct from
'becoming'; it could also mean a rich man's property.
Hypostasis, besides 'real nature', could mean support,
foundation, confidence, ambush, abscess and sediment.
Which of these meanings did the trinitarian use imply? It is
not surprising that it was originally uncertain whether, as
trinitarian terms, *ousia* and *hypostasis* meant the same or
were sharply contrasted, and if the latter, which of them
the Latin word *substantia* translated![1]

1. In the anathemas appended to the original creed of Nicea *hypostasis*
    and *ousia* are identified, and it is forbidden to say that the Son is of
    another *hypostasis* or *ousia* (ie from the Father). This was offensive

The existence of terms like this heightens the need for an analogy which will control the way they are used. Technical terms which can be given a precise meaning are useful and necessary, but they may not mean much to ordinary people. Concrete analogies and sermon illustrations are popular but likely to be misunderstood. The question was, could Christianity find an analogy of the Trinity concrete enough to appeal to ordinary people without being seriously misleading? The quest covers the entire Christian era.

Analogies from the inanimate or the impersonal are of small value. But from at least the fourth century, orthodox terminology described God as 'three persons', and two of these are (on the highest authority) 'Father' and 'Son'. As indicated in the last chapter, this suggests the obvious analogy of three human beings, always with the proviso that they are united in such a way as to make them 'One God'.

Such a line of thought commended itself to many of the Eastern Fathers, and, with qualifications, to Augustine of Hippo. Human experience, he said, discloses a trinity of the lover, the person or object beloved, and the love that binds them.[2] It should be remembered that Augustine did not put this forward as a direct or primary analogy of the Trinity, but as an analysis of the concept of love which gives us a glimpse of the nature of God who is Love (I John 4:8). Its success for trinitarian theology depends on the concept of 'person'. If this is taken in the developed modern sense, it becomes two independent people and an

---

to many in the Greek-speaking East, because it seemed to them to deny any real distinction between the Father and the Son (the mistake of 'Sabellianism'). Athanasius subsequently reconciled East and West by contradicting this and saying that Father, Son and Spirit *are* three separate *hypostases* (= *personae*, persons); but they are one *ousia*, translated by the Latin word *substantia* (substance), though grammatically *substantia* is the exact equivalent of *hypostasis*! With this qualification most of the Church accepted that the Father, Son and Spirit are one *ousia, homo-ousios*, consubstantial.

2. *De Trinitate*, XV, 5; XV, 10.

abstract idea; a disastrous analogy.[3] But if it is persons in the 'lower' sense (as in Chapter 3) where two are required for full 'personality' and their love is the completing third dimension of their unity, it may well serve.

Augustine, however, as we have already seen, himself marks a significant movement in the concepts of individuality and personality. He had a life-long fascination for the correspondence between God the Holy Trinity and the individual human being. He was not the first thinker to put forward the 'psychological analogy', as this correspondence may be called. He was anticipated, and influenced, by Victorinus Afer, a Latin philosopher converted to Christianity in the middle of the fourth century. Victorinus perceived that man is a complex being, having both a secret core and self-expression, which he took to be the human analogies of the Father and the Son. But Victorinus, obscure in expression at the best of times,[4] is not able to give the analogy satisfactory completion in relation to the Spirit.

Augustine was a much greater theologian than Victorinus, and he brings to the task his sensitive awareness of human personality. He considers the human soul to consist of memory, understanding and will, this triune structure being true both within itself and in relation to other souls and God. These three terms constitute a 'psychological analogy' with the Holy Trinity.[5]

Augustine is very modest about his analogy; and it must be admitted that, as a development of Victorinus, it goes in the wrong direction. His aspects of the soul do not correspond to particular divine persons. Moreover, do these aspects exhaust the soul? What about emotion, or activity? As an analogy of the *Trinity* it is very limited, as Augustine was the first to admit.

There may be discoverable reasons for this. To a biblical

3. See W.R. Matthews, *God in Christian Thought and Experience*, Nisbet, 3rd Edition 1963, p.195.
4. See P. Henry and P. Hadot, *Sources Chrétiennes*, Vols. 58 and 59, Editions du Cerf, 1960.
5. *De Trinitate*, IX, 2-8; X, 17-19, XIV, 11-end.

horror of idolatry Augustine added a dread of pride and an asceticism which owed much to the Platonic tradition. His heightened sense of personality had not matured sufficiently to make it fully usable for this purpose. So the psychological analogy, sketched by Victorinus and misdirected by Augustine, lay dormant for centuries.

It reappears, brief but complete, on the threshold of the present century, in R.C. Moberly's *Atonement and Personality* (Murray, 1901). Seeking a triune structure of human personality, Moberly writes,

> First, then, there is the man as he really is in himself, invisible, indeed, and inaccessible,—and yet, directly, the fountain, origin, and cause of everything that can be called in any sense himself. Secondly, there is himself as projected into conditions of visibleness,—the overt expression or utterance of himself. This, under the conditions of our actual experience, will mean for the most part his expression or image as body,—the touch of his hand, the tone of his voice, the shining of his eye, the utterance of his words: all, in a word, that makes up, to us, that outward expression of himself, which we call himself, and which he himself ordinarily recognizes as the very mirror and image and reality of himself. And thirdly, there is the reply of what we call external nature to him—his operation or effect.[6]

The paragraph, like the book in which it appears, 'stands apart with a certain loneliness'.[7] Moberly was modest about his analogy and, in the spirit of Augustine, points out its limitations. He is looking for analogies of the Spirit, and omits to say that the inner self and the revealed self are analogies of the Father and the Son, though it cannot be doubted that such was his intention. He gives no source, and never refers to the analogy elsewhere in any of his published works. His son, Bishop R.H. Moberly, could recall no development of the idea by his father. Moberly,

---

6. p.174.
7. A.M. Ramsey, *From Gore to Temple*, Longmans, 1960, p.46.

said[8] to be a deep thinker rather than a wide reader, seems to have produced the analogy by meditating on Victorinus and Augustine. Certainly his friend Charles Gore wrote the only considerable article on Victorinus in English, in the *Dictionary of Christian Biography*, 1887.[9]

Little notice was taken of Moberly's analogy. But in 1937 the detective novelist Dorothy L. Sayers wrote a play for the Canterbury Festival (about William of Sens and the building of the Cathedral) called *The Zeal of Thy House*. At the end, St. Michael makes this speech:

> Praise Him that He hath made man in His own image, a maker and craftsman like Himself, a little mirror of His triune majesty.
> For every work of creation is threefold, an earthly trinity to match the heavenly.
> First: there is the Creative Idea; passionless, timeless, beholding the whole work complete at once, the end in the beginning; and this is the image of the Father.
> Second: there is the Creative Energy, begotten of that Idea, working in time from the beginning to the end, with sweat and passion, being incarnate in the bonds of matter, and this is the image of the Word.
> Third: there is the Creative Power, the meaning of the work and its response in the lively soul; and this is the image of the indwelling Spirit.
> And these three are one, each equally in itself the whole work, whereof none can exist without other; and this is the image of the Trinity.[10]

Sayers, for all her admiration of St Augustine, did not share his diffidence; she has the combative and controversial confidence of another trinitarian theologian, Peter Abelard.[11] What she has done is easily apparent. She has

---

8. By W. Sanday in his memoir in J.T.S. 1903.
9. The extent of the modern knowledge of Victorinus may be indicated by the fact that when I wished to read this in Exeter University Library a few years ago, I had to cut the pages.
10. Dorothy L. Sayers, *Four Sacred Plays*, Gollancz, 1948, p.103.
11. She had a personal circumstance in common with Augustine and Abelard, as readers of the recent biographies will know.

shifted the trinitarian analogy from the human person to the human work. In *The Mind of the Maker*, (Methuen, 1941), her most considerable theological writing, she provides an extended commentary on her version of the analogy. In making the shift she has drawn on ideas of human creativity derived from G.K. Chesterton, whom she frequently mentions.

Gilbert Keith Chesterton (1874-1936), journalist, poet and essayist, was, during Sayers's youth and period of detective writing, a prominent lay defender of Christian orthodoxy. He was a detective writer himself. His detective, Father Brown, a Roman Catholic priest, ranks among the best-known heroes of English crime fiction.

Chesterton was also a machine-hating Romantic looking for the re-creation of the sort of England he supposed to have existed in the Middle Ages—an England of peasant farmers and craftsmen. Much of Chesterton's history (and even more that of his friend Hilaire Belloc) is highly imaginative and his economic and social expectations were unpractical. But his favourite doctrine of man as himself a creator, made in the image of God, already had a long history.

It cannot be said to be prominent in the Bible, where 'the work of men's hands'[12] commonly means the idol, the image of a false God made by men, and fear of idolatry prevented the development of a doctrine of man as a creator. In the Greek classical tradition, which contributed much to early Christianity, the greatest sin was pride, in the sense of a claim by man to exercise the power and pre-rogative of the gods. This also inhibited a doctrine of human creativity. These two fears—of idolatry and pride—dominated the early Christian centuries, and go far to explain the lack of any appeal to human creativity in the trinitarian analogies of Victorinus and Augustine.

But after its first millenium western Christianity became more confident about man. The Cistercian movement, which flourished in the twelfth century, attributed to the labours of the illiterate lay-brothers (the *conversi*) the same

12. Psalm 115:4.

value as the worship offered by the choir monks. The one was *opus dei* (the work of God) as much as the other— *laborare est orare*. Then radical elements in the friar movements, like the Dominicans Eckhart (1260-1327) and Tauler (1300-61) applied this idea more generally to lay life, and it became the philosophy of the craft guilds, with momentous results.[13]

An indication of its popularity and acceptance is provided by the Tumbler corbel in Exeter Cathedral. This illustrates the story of the acrobat who went into a monastery but found he had no aptitude for monastic worship and meditation, so he privately followed his old trade before the statue of Our Lady, who miraculously accepted his offering in spite of the disapproval of the other monks. The date of the corbel is about 1330.

Chesterton, who had no particular contribution to make on the doctrine of the Trinity, nevertheless clearly held that there was an analogy between human literary work and God's creation. Introducing his own poetry, he wrote,

> Another tattered rhymester in the ring,
>   With but the old plea to the sneering schools,
> That on him too, some secret night in spring,
>   Came the old frenzy of a hundred fools
>
> To make some thing: the old want dark and deep,
>   The thirst of men, the hunger of the stars,
> Since first it tinged even th'Eternal's sleep,
>   With monstrous dreams of trees and towns
>   and wars.
>
> When all He made for the first time He saw,
>   Scattering stars as misers shake their pelf,
> Then in the last strange wrath broke His own law,
>   And made a graven image of himself.[14]

13. 'From the craft guild ethic stems the driving power of the Reformation, Capitalism, Democracy and Socialism. Although they took diverse intellectual forms, all these movements derive their *passion* from the craft guild ethic. The passion, the master-idea ... is that work is good and idleness is shameful.' W.P. Witcutt, *The Rise and Fall of the Individual*, SPCK, 1958.

It was Dorothy L. Sayers's achievement to combine this Chestertonian restatement of a familiar Christian theme with the unique and isolated insight of Moberly, which she had at first hand or at some unknown second hand.[15] For a major insight into the mystery of the Trinity to have been achieved by two rather odd detective novelists may perhaps be taken as a latter-day example of God choosing what is foolish in the world to shame the wise (1 Corinthians 1:27).

14.   *The Wild Knight,* 1900.
15.   See Appendix: 'Missing Link', p.77.

CHAPTER EIGHT

God and Man

'You feel you never know the man himself.' 'He's putting on an act.' 'He's not what he appears to be.' Such judgements are often made and heard; the final one perhaps in the first person. If we are considering, not a man's relations with others but his own integrity, we might say, 'He doesn't really understand himself', or 'He hasn't come to terms with himself.'

Such language shows that, in our practical understanding of human personality, we assume a distinction of persons (in the trinitarian sense of the word); a distinction between the inner self and the revealed self. Their failure to tally occasions moral judgements. But the distinction does not depend on sin. If someone 'puts his personality over' or 'expresses himself well' we recognize the unity and harmony of the inner and revealed self without denying the distinction.[1]

1. The distinction between the inner and revealed self of a man forms part of the teaching of Jesus in the synoptic gospels. See St. Matthew 12:33-35 (cf. St. Luke 6:43-45), where 'treasure' and 'heart' is Jesus's way of speaking of the inner self. For the disharmony of inner and revealed self, see St. Matthew 7:15, the 'wolf in sheep's clothing'.

In his portrayal of human personality and human sin in
The Great Divorce, C.S. Lewis presents one of his ghosts
as two 'people'.

> While we spoke the Lady was steadily advancing
> towards us, but it was not at us she looked. Follow-
> ing the direction of her eyes, I turned and saw an
> oddly-shaped phantom approaching, or rather two
> phantoms: a great tall Ghost, horribly thin and
> shaky, who seemed to be leading on a chain another
> Ghost no bigger than an organ-grinder's monkey.
> The taller Ghost ... was like a seedy actor of the old
> school ...
> Then I noticed two things ... first, the little Ghost
> was not being led by the big one. It was the dwarfish
> figure that held the chain in his hand and the theatri-
> cal figure that wore the collar round its neck. In the
> second place, I noticed that the Lady was looking
> solely at the dwarf Ghost ... 'You missed me?' he
> croaked in a small bleating voice ...
> What happened next gave me a shock. The Dwarf
> and the Tragedian spoke in unison, not to her but to
> one another. 'You'll notice', they warned one
> another, 'she hasn't answered our question.' I realised
> then that they were one person, or rather that both
> were the remains of what had once been a person.[2]

Lewis is not here concerned with trinitarian theology.
He is presenting in a vivid pictorial way the effect of sin on
the human personality. In this case, what is left is the inner
self (the Dwarf) and the revealed self (the Actor), disas-
trously at odds with each other, though sometimes col-
laborating against the outside world. The good and loving
Lady sees, indeed sees exclusively, the inner self, and
though it is not at the moment very lovable, she would
save it, if only it would abandon the destructive and false
revealed self which is its damnation and eventually con-
sumes it entirely. We are accustomed to various portrayals
of the 'persons' of the Holy Trinity. It is valuable and

2. *The Great Divorce*, Bles, 1945, pp.99-109.

instructive to have for contrast and comparison this rare, perhaps unique, word-picture of the 'persons' in man.

The modern use of the word 'image' provides another pointer in the same direction. In his first government Harold Wilson projected, so his advisers felt, the wrong image—one of interfering omnicompetence—and this was deliberately changed. Churchmen are often worried about the Church's image as old-fashioned and introverted, and make unconvincing forays in the direction of modernity.

If your image does you less than justice you suffer, as Queen Mary I has suffered in English history under the image of 'Bloody Mary', when she could easily lay claim to have been the most honest and benevolent monarch of the century. The opposite is true of her half-sister Elizabeth I, whose reign was a skilful image projection with remarkably little behind it. Propaganda, press and personal determination can make a laudatory image. But if people succeed in penetrating below (or at least to a truer image), as they did with President Nixon, then the image-projector may incur that most damning of modern criticisms, insincerity.

Scholars of a certain type frequently tell us how alien to our understanding are biblical and patristic categories of thought, and no doubt this is often true. But the language of *image* seems something which, though the ancients used, they understood less well, in human terms, than we do; no doubt because of our developed understanding of human personality. The language of *image* takes us straight to the doctrine of the Trinity, where the Son or Word is the image of the Father and the way the Father reveals or expresses himself. 'For us men and for our salvation', this is done in the incarnation. For God to create man in his image is to move towards incarnation. But, in himself and apart from creation, God begets his Son, his image, from all eternity, and beholds, knows and loves himself therein.

To be distinct without disharmony is the mark of the Father and the Son, both in biblical and patristic understanding. This is what the Christ of St. John's Gospel expresses;[3] their unity: 'I and the Father are one' (John 10:30), 'He who has seen me has seen the Father ... I am in the Father and the Father in me' (John 14:9ff); their love;

'The Father loves the Son' (John 5:20), 'I love the Father' (John 14:31); and the primacy of the Father: 'The Father is greater than I' (John 14:28), 'The Son can do nothing of himself' (John 5:19).

The psychological analogy does not end here. The man who expresses himself, 'puts himself over ', projects his image, does something to which others must relate. He writes a book, makes a speech, preaches a sermon. But his self-expression is not effective unless others see and understand. His idea must flow through them and back to himself; otherwise the self-expression is still-born.

Even within himself a man must do this. He must project the image of himself for himself, and so know and love himself.[4] This love and knowledge complete his trinity of being, as Augustine claimed for his analogy of the Lover and the Beloved. The third person might be called the effective self,[5] and it is not at all easy to examine apart from the other two. Its absence or weakness means disharmony, in-

---

3. Modern biblical criticism usually considers that St. John's Gospel is late (around AD 100) and inferior to the other three as a report of the *verba ipsissima* of Jesus. Its characteristic language is thought to be Christian reflection on the person and status of Jesus. But *no* gospel datings rest on firm evidence, and a powerful minority of scholars claim that St. John is not significantly later than the others, and is in some ways superior as history. See J.A.T. Robinson, *Redating the New Testament*, SCM, 1976, Chapter IX. St. John's Father-Son language is so startling and radical that, if not due to Jesus, it presumes an unknown mind as great as, if not greater than, his—a difficult hypothesis. May it not be suggested that St. John's language is genuine reminiscence which St. Mark, for reasons obscure to us, reported in 'Son of Man' terms? See above, Chapter 3.

4. Here the human analogy corresponds to what theologians call the 'essential' Trinity. Where relations with other persons are in view, the correspondence is with the 'economic' Trinity. 'Essential' describes God 'as he exists in his own eternal being', and 'economic' describes him 'as he reveals himself in the process of creation and redemption'—J.N.D. Kelly, *Early Christian Doctrines*, A. & C. Black, 1960, p.110.

5. The effective self corresponds closely to 'fruits' in the teaching of Jesus—fruits which indicate both the quality of the inner self and also the truth of the image; see St. Matthew 7:16-20.

effectiveness, boredom. But, on the other hand, when present it points away from itself to the harmony of inner self and image.

The effective self is the analogy of the third person of the Holy Trinity, the Holy Spirit. God reveals his inner self to us; the Father sends the Son. But the divine plan and action is not complete until we respond and our response is God effective in and through us, the Holy Spirit. 'No-one can say Jesus is Lord, except by the Holy Spirit' (1 Corinthians 12:3). But the Spirit diverts attention from himself and turns it to the Father and the Son. Jesus says of him, 'He will glorify me, for everything that he makes known to you he will draw from what is mine' (John 16:14). He is the eye which sees, and in consequence the one thing that cannot directly be seen. This is why hymns and prayers addressed to the Spirit are never very satisfactory. It is the Son who is the image of the Father and the visual focus of devotion. To try to turn our response to the image into another objective focus is to make the Spirit, in effect, a title of Christ. There may be no great harm in that, so long as we recognize what we are doing, and realize that the difficulty of objectivising the Spirit authenticates, rather than discredits, the doctrine.

Man, therefore, is the analogy of God because both are an inner, a revealed and an effective self. The Trinity of God is perfect, a Trinity of unity and love, without division of substance or confusion of persons. The trinity of man is lopsided and scalene, his being divided and his selves confused. But he is still a trinity, made in the likeness of God whose unity and perfection is his goal.

CHAPTER NINE

Creative Mind

One form of the psychological analogy has received extended treatment—that produced by Dorothy L. Sayers as the basis of her theology. Her book, *The Mind of the Maker* (1941), is of overwhelming importance for the analogy of the Trinity. But various factors, like the date of publication, the author's fame as a detective novelist, and the prominence in the book of literary criticism, have diminished its theological impact.

Sayers analyses the creative work, or the act of creation, into Idea, Activity[1] and Power, and relates these to the three divine persons. Exploring Moberly's analogy (as Moberly does not himself do) is an exercise in moral psychology. The Sayers analogy, if developed in terms of work in general, would be very similar. But as applied to a particular form of artistic creation, its details are technical or literary criticism. She herself expounds the analogy mainly in terms of novels and plays, and this has a three-fold advantage. First, it is her own discipline. She had a dozen Wimsey novels to her credit, and a number of plays,

1. The term she came to prefer for 'Energy'.

including the epoch-making wireless play cycle, *The Man Born to be King*. Second, the novelist and playwright must create his own world—a particularly useful analogy for God's creation. And third, creation in words is particularly appropriate as the analogy of God who creates and reveals by his Word, especially his Word-made-Flesh. Doubtless other forms of human activity are subject to the Trinitarian analogy.[2] But without words they may be more difficult to explore.

Some definition must be given of the three terms, which, it will be noticed, correspond to the three-fold structure both of Moberly's analogy and to plan, event and memory (Chapter 4). Idea, Activity and Power are not to be taken in a philosophical or scientific sense, but 'in the sense intended by the poet and the common man'.[3] Thus a writer will say, 'I have an idea for a book', and such an Idea logically precedes any mental or physical work on materials. Yet even the formulation of the Idea in the mind is not the Idea itself, but an awareness of it in the Activity. So the Idea does not precede the Activity in time, just as the Son is not temporally prior to the Father, but 'eternally begotten'. The human creator formulating his Idea to himself, without putting pen to paper, is the analogy of the essential Trinity,[4] where God eternally knows and loves himself, and is under no necessity to create anything in particular.

Since we can never isolate the Idea, how do we know it has any real existence? Since we can know the Father only through the Son, how can we be sure there *is* a Father? In the latter case, the Son is very positive about it. In the

2. See Chapter 4, note 5.
3. *The Mind of the Maker*, p.28, note 1.
4. For 'essential Trinity' see Chapter 8, note 4. Of the human writer's Idea, Activity and Power, Sayers writes, 'These three are equally and eternally present in his own act of creation, and at every moment of it, whether or not the act ever becomes manifest in the form of a written and printed book... The whole complex relation ... may remain entirely within the sphere of the imagination, and is there complete. The Trinity abides and works and is responsive to itself "in Heaven" ', (*The Mind of the Maker*, p.31).

former, the Activity is conscious of referring all acts and choices to an existing and complete whole. There is a powerful sense that the book already exists. It is the business of the Activity to discover it, to embody and incarnate it.

The Activity is, as the analogy would lead us to expect, the easiest of the three to grasp. Like the incarnate Son, it is the only one apparent to the senses. The Activity is in fact everything that translates the Idea into material and communicable form. If it is a book, it is the whole business of formulating it in the mind and putting pen to paper, typing, researching, checking, correcting, publishing, printing, proof-reading, marketing; and the book as a material object which can be read, ignored, rudely reviewed, lost, burnt or put on the Index.

The Power is what flows back to the author from his own Activity and makes him a reader of his own book; so that even within himself he can say, 'Yes, I see; the Idea is revealed to me through my own Activity; I respond and rejoice.' But once in tangible form it communicates the Idea to others and produces the response of power in them. We commonly (and quite rightly) identify the whole book with its *power*—its effect on its readers; although, given the imperfection of both readers and writer, this effect is by no means always what the writer consciously intended.

Sayers has much to say about both Christian doctrine and literary criticism which go beyond the scope of this present study.[5] But we may note how the analogy can be applied to human work in general where there is an imbalance among the three terms Idea (Father), Activity (Son), and Power (Ghost). The most recognizable form has one to excess, and the other two consequently deficient.

The 'Father-ridden' is the man who could have done great things but circumstances were always against him. The existence of an Idea, given some preliminary formulation as he sat in his armchair or enjoyed a quiet drink, seemed all that was necessary; indeed, others should be

5. See J.A. Thurmer, 'The Theology of Dorothy L. Sayers', in *Church Quarterly Review*, 1967.

able to recognize and accept it without the tiresome process of explaining it to them. In ordinary terms, the Father-ridden is arrogant and idle.

The Son-ridden, on the other hand, is everlastingly busy rushing around in a hectic Activity which exhibits no overmastering Idea, and so (like the Father-ridden, with whom he has this at least in common) there is no real return of Power. He is not lazy, but he is liable to a breakdown.

The Ghost-ridden has no creative Idea to put over, but expects a response as a thing-in-itself. So a weak comedian will try to build his act simply on the audience's willingness to be amused, and the grinning cleric will beam and have a lilt in his voice even when he speaks words of doom and damnation.

Some aspects of the modern charismatic movement might incur the charge of being Ghost-ridden by their emphasis on things which are properly a response to the love of the Father mediated through the Son. Indeed, if we were to offer charismatics a homely proverb, it might be, 'Look after the Father and the Son, and the Spirit will look after himself.'

CHAPTER TEN

Christ the Trinity

In *The Mind of the Maker* Dorothy L. Sayers uses her version of the psychological analogy to illuminate various areas of Christian doctrine—creation, free will, miracle and the problem of evil. On the analogy of the human writer, the incarnation corresponds to autobiography,[1] and the correspondence leads to a triumphant vindication of catholic doctrine.

> [An autobiography] appears with a double nature, 'divine and human'; the whole story is contained within the mind of its maker, but the mind of the maker is also imprisoned within the story and cannot escape from it. It is 'altogether God', in that it is the sole arbiter of the form the story is to take, and yet 'altogether man' in that, having created the form, it is bound to display itself in conformity with the nature of that form. ... By incarnation, the creator says in effect, 'See! this is what my eternal Idea looks like in terms of my own creation; this is my manhood ... this is my characterhood in a volume of created characters' (pp.71, 72).

1. Chapters 7 and 9.

But Sayers does not use the analogy to pursue the more technical aspects of Christology. Can it shed any light on controversies ancient or modern? It is often said that the great debate about Jesus, divine and human, which raged in the church of the late fourth and fifth centuries, received less successful resolution than the earlier question of the Trinity, partly because there were no minds as great as Athanasius and Augustine to apply themselves to it. Cyril of Alexandria (d.444), in combating his enemy Nestorius, developed the doctrine of *anhypostasia*, usually translated 'impersonal humanity', and often regarded as a repellent, if not self-contradictory, conception. The 'personality' of Jesus, said Cyril, was the *Logos;* otherwise Jesus would be two persons, which was what Nestorius was accused of saying. Cyril's doctrine on this point was confirmed by the Council of Chalcedon, 451, which proclaimed Christ 'in two natures, without confusion, without change, without division, without separation . . . each nature . . . coming together to form one person . . . not as parted or separated into two persons'.

The Christological question was, and usually still is, discussed in isolation from the Trinity. It is posed as the relation between the second divine person, the *Logos* or Word, and the human Jesus, without significant reference to the Father or the Spirit. The original reason for this was that it was mainly an eastern controversy, and although the 'Nicene' creed had been accepted, it was interpreted in the most 'pluralistic' way possible. The incarnation was the business of the Son or Word, and the other two Persons could be largely ignored. So separate considerations of the Trinity and the Incarnation became standard in Christian thought.

But the analogy asserts very strongly the unity of God, with Jesus as the expressive being, or activity, *of God*. The separation of Christology from the Trinity creates unnecessary categories. The Word was made flesh—that is, human, with body, mind and (human) spirit. But the Word is the Father's Word, inseparable from him. So the 'inmost being' of Jesus is not so much the eternal *Logos* as the Father, just as his effective being is the divine Spirit.[2]

Now it is essential to the Moberly analogy that a man has an 'inner being' which, like the rest of him, is created. Jesus has an inner being which is divine and not human; that is where his humanity differs from ours.[3] If we say, 'Then Jesus is not human', that depends on what we mean by human. Much modern thought on this subject seems to take it for granted that we know all about humanity, and about 'being human', and we will fit Jesus into it if we can, though our efforts often make him sound like a conundrum or a monster. This, from any seriously Christian standpoint, is the most arrant presumption. Quite apart from the technicalities of Christian doctrine, it was as a man that Jesus made his original impact, and as a man that he continues to make a unique appeal to the mind and

---

2. We may note the baptism of Jesus, when the Father's voice acknowledges the Son, and the Spirit appears as a dove (Mark 1:10,11); and traditional representations of the crucifixion, where the Father is a hand and the Spirit again a dove. 'The pictures of the First and Third Persons are pure intellectual symbol—they represent nothing in time-space-matter; but the picture of the Second Person is living symbol: it represents an event in history. This is what our analogy would lead us to expect' (*The Mind of the Maker*, pp.98-99). At the same time, Sayers could appreciate the value of sometimes representing the Trinity as three identical men ('The Trinity in the mind'), and here her insight is better than great authorities like Calvin and Barth with their humourless rejection of 'trois marmousets'. (Barth, op.cit., p.411). See also Chapter 2, note 8.

3. E. Brunner, discussing the incarnation without relation to the Trinity, reaches a similar conclusion. A human being has 'a mystery of personality, which is in no wise identical with his historical personality ... which is visible to the historian or the biographer'. In Jesus the 'mystery of the Person' is divine; his historical personality is human (*The Mediator*, E.T. Lutterworth, 1934, pp.318-319). Brunner's point is not refuted by D.M. Baillie's somewhat hysterical criticism (*God was in Christ*, Faber, 1948, p.89). Brunner (and Moberly) may be indebted to psychology's 'transcendental ego' and 'empirical ego'; why not? And even if it were true that 'each is sheer abstraction when separated from the other' human thought would not get far without abstractions. Baillie's own idea is that Christ's humanity has no personality *independent of God*. But 'independent of God' must mean human or created. So his doctrine is indistinguishable from those he attacks. If they are Apollinarian (i.e. without true humanity) so is he.

heart of half the world. Might it not be reasonable, on those grounds alone, to suppose that the rest of humanity should be measured by him, and not the other way round? Christian theology, when it tries to define the humanity of Jesus, is apt to come up with definitions like 'impersonal humanity' which sound alien, and which seem to cut him off from the rest of us. But, in a sense, he *is* cut off from the rest of us, whether we like it or not. His unique conscious-ness of the Father and the Spirit, and the place he occupies in human history, *do* 'cut him off'.

Yet what is apt to sound alien and 'inhuman' is the goal of spiritual development to which all Christians are com-mitted. It is the object of our discipleship to attune our inner being to God—'thy will be done'—and so to have our effective being filled with, or possessed by, the Holy Spirit. If the doctrine of the incarnation has suffered from isolation from that of the Trinity, it has suffered also from lack of connection with the language of sanctification and spirituality. We are always told, and may gladly believe, that the achievement of our spiritual destiny does not make us cease to be human; rather, it is the true humanity. The whole life of Jesus exhibits the true humanity to which the rest of us feebly aspire. True humanity *needs* an inner and an effective being which is divine. Jesus has it by right, the rest of us have it by 'adoption and grace'. May not this application of the analogy shed light on something like 'impersonal humanity', which sounds so off-putting?

Jesus in the gospels never speaks, as later theology so often does, of the relation of his humanity to the Divine Word or *Logos*. He speaks frequently of his relation to the Father and the Spirit. If we took him seriously we could profess an orthodoxy more radical than much conven-tional Christian thought, 'orthodox' or not.

It may be objected that the Divine Word, incarnate 'without remainder', smacks of doctrines of 'self-emptying', *Kenosis*[4], which appealed to a number of nineteenth- and

4. The noun cognate with the verb which St. Paul uses in Philippians 2:7, where it is likely that it refers not to the divine Word taking flesh, but to the human Jesus renouncing in the Passion the dominion of unfallen Adam.

twentieth-century Christians as a way of explaining the
true humanity of Jesus. Metaphysical attributes like omnipotence, omniscience and impassibility[5] must, it is said,
have been shed by the Word in the process of the incarnation. The idea has philosophical difficulties. How much
can God 'give up' and still be God? Modern theological
journals are full of articles by philosophers telling us what
God, as God, cannot do.

But just as our knowledge of humanity is limited and fal-
lible, so the meaning of the metaphysical attributes is far
from clear or obvious. Does omnipotence mean God can
do anything? Can he make good evil, and evil good? Is
good good because God says so or is its goodness something independent which God recognises? This was one of
the great arguments of the medieval schoolmen, and we
may profess agnosticism as to whether God *cannot*, or *will
not* do evil. The important thing is, he does not; he is faithful and 'cannot deny himself'.

God does all things, knows all things, and suffers all
things which are consistent with his being and nature. That
being and nature is Trinity in Unity, expression of himself
to himself and to other beings in love. To be incarnate in
order to express himself to man made in his image is self-
fulfilment, not self-emptying. And it is in Jesus that the
metaphysical attributes are given definition. He can, and
does, heal the sick, quell the storm, raise the dead; he does
everything the Father wills. He knows the Father and he
knows what is in man. He suffers nothing but what is
written of him, and even that in his own time and by his
own (and the Father's) will.

It may be objected that what we have done is to convert
the Godhead of the Eternal Word into flesh, whereas the
Athanasian Creed [6] says that Christ's unity comes 'not by
conversion of Godhead into flesh; but by taking manhood
into God'. But the *Quicunque* makes perfectly good sense
if we take the unity of the Godhead seriously. To think of

5. Ability to do everything; knowing everything; immunity from pain
   and suffering.
6. *Quicunque vult*, a fifth-century canticle embodying St. Augustine's
   doctrine of the Trinity and the Incarnation. See Appendix B.

the Father and the Spirit being 'converted into flesh' offends both orthodoxy and sense. It is God the Trinity, in the 'person' of the Son or Word who 'takes the manhood into God' where it abides for ever.

The Athanasian Creed has been much criticized ever since the rationalist and 'unitarian' movements of the eighteenth century. Its confident assertion of a thorough-going Augustinian trinitarianism, with damnation for objectors (v.2 and v.42) gave, and continues to give, offence. Can salvation depend on performing mental gymnastics?

The Creed is vulnerable, but its weakness is not where rationalists and liberals have thought. Its poetic, almost playful, balancing of the One and the Three (vv.3-27) is an accurate verbal diagram of the divine mystery, and the damnatory clauses are surely true in this sense, that to believe, *fully and with all one's being*, the Catholic faith and to be saved are the same thing. Can anyone be saved unless *in the end* he holds the Catholic faith? As Sayers characteristically observed, ' "Except a man believe rightly he cannot"—at any rate, his artistic structure cannot possibly—"be saved" '.[7]

The weakness of the Creed is the way it keeps the Trinity and the Incarnation separate. It deals with the Trinity (vv.3-28) without mentioning the Incarnation, and then deals with the Incarnation (vv.29-41) with no mention of the Trinity, apart from references to the Father in vv.31, 33 and 39. There is no reference to the Spirit at all. The Father and the Spirit do not appear to be concerned, in any dynamic way, with the Son's incarnation.

The ancient baptismal creeds, represented by the 'Apostles" and the Eucharistic, or 'Nicene' creeds, are much sounder.[8] Their three-fold structure corresponds to the three Persons, and the historical incarnation is dealt with in the second and central section. In this way the Trinity is anchored for us in space and time, and the incarnation exhibits the Trinity.

7. *The Man Born to be King*, Gollancz, 1943, Introduction p.19.
8. See Appendix B.

The second half of the Athanasian Creed is notable also for containing an 'official' recognition of the psychological analogy—v.37. 'For as reasoning soul and flesh is one man: so God and man is one Christ.' This is an analogy, not between man and God, but between man and Christ. Moreover, the structure of it suggests that 'soul' in man corresponds to 'God' in Christ, and that therefore Christ's soul was divine. But that explanation cannot be intended; it was the view of Apollinarius, and condemned by the Council of Constantinople in 381. This reduces the teaching of the verse to the rather general truth that the existence of distinct elements in Christ do not destroy his unity, any more than the existence of distinct elements in any and every man destroys his.[9] We recall that the furthest Augustine's analogy of the Trinity goes is to indicate that man is a complex being, with perhaps a tripartite complexity.

The Athanasian Creed is right to draw attention to the significance of man for the understanding of the divine. Its unfortunate division between the Trinity and the Incarnation makes it unable to develop that significance, and reduces its own value, here and at other points of its teaching.

---

9. 'The one and only point to which attention is drawn is the way in which, without losing their separate identity, two distinct substances are united in man so as to form one individual, a single person.' J.N.D. Kelly, *The Athanasian Creed*, A. & C. Black, 1964.

CHAPTER ELEVEN

The Paraclete

As we said in Chapter 2, considerable importance attaches to the choice between translating or simply transliterating a word in an ancient language. St. John's word for the Holy Spirit (John 14:16; 16:7, etc.) has variously been translated 'Comforter', 'Counsellor' or 'Advocate'; but these words as used elsewhere probably contribute little to our understanding, and there is much to be said for simply anglicizing the Greek word to serve as a title of the elusive Spirit. How effectively J.M. Neale introduced it into his translation of the Latin hymn *Veni sancte Spiritus*, though it was not in the original:

> Come thou holy Paraclete
> And from thy celestial seat
> Send thy light and brilliancy.[1]

It is understandable that theological definition of the Spirit should have been delayed until the church had

1. English Hymnal 155.

cleared its mind about the role of the Son. Both in
Christian theology and in the analogies we have pursued,
the third term, the Spirit, the effective self, the power,
require a degree of self-conscious reflection to be identified
and distinguished from the other terms. The Church never
had a major controversy about the Spirit, as it did about
the Son.

Yet, curiously, the one formal difference between the
trinitarian doctrines of the main eastern and western
traditions concerns the Spirit. The original text of the
eucharistic creed, common to east and west, echoed John
15:26 and ran, 'I believe in the Holy Ghost, the Lord, the
Life-Giver, who proceeds from the Father ...'. To this
western usage appended from about the sixth century 'and
(from) the Son', in Latin, *Filioque*. The addition is not
accepted by the eastern churches, partly because the original text was promulgated by ecumenical councils which
alone would be competent to make alterations; partly
because it is thought to be wrong or dubious in itself.

Modern ecumenical contacts have produced considerable
sympathy in the west for the eastern point of view, and
suggestions are made that the *Filioque* clause should be
dropped or made optional. At the enthronement of the
Archbishop of Canterbury (R.A.K. Runcie) in 1980 the
creed was used without it, no doubt as a gesture to the
Orthodox present.

But there are considerations other than those of church
unity in this matter. The *Church Times*, once the
aggressive upholder of credal orthodoxy, in welcoming the
usage of the Archbishop's enthronement, referred to the
Filioque as 'this obscure point' [2], implying thereby that we
cannot really know the relation of the Spirit to the Father
and the Son.

Such a degree of agnosticism appeals at the present time
to a good many leaders of Christian life and thought. An
example of it is provided by the recent article 'And From
the Son?' by the Bishop of Birmingham (H. Montefiore) in

2. 30 May 1980.

the magazine *Theology*.[3] The clause, he says, purports to describe the *origin* of the Spirit, 'a matter about which Christians can have no direct knowledge.... There are those who say his origins in eternity must be similar to the way in which we know him in the world—from the Father through the Son—*but this is by no means clear*' (my italics). This combines two errors. The first error is like that of the Arians mentioned in Chapter 3. They thought that 'begotten' as applied to the Eternal Son was based on the analogy of the human act of begetting, when in fact it is based on the *relationship* of a father and adult son. It is suggested here that 'proceeding' as applied to the Eternal Spirit describes origin in time or pseudo-time, when, once again, it describes relationship. Where, however, the Arians were just wrong and misunderstood the analogy, Montefiore adds the further error of denying that any analogy can be appealed to. This oversteps that vital boundary where agnosticism ceases to be reticence and humility and becomes unbelief. The Son, in space and time, reveals the Father and sends the Spirit, exhibiting thereby the eternal Trinity. No doubt it is true that we can know the 'essential' Trinity only through the 'economic' Trinity.[4] But what is so known and revealed is true of God's eternal being. That is what it means to call God 'faithful'. If this were not so, then analogy—including the enacted analogy of the incarnation—could tell us nothing about God, and there would be no basis for theology (activity or magazine) and no point in Bishops (of Birmingham or anywhere else).

The Moberly-Sayers analogy strongly supports the *Filioque*,[5] though 'through the Son' might be better. A man's operation of effect certainly proceeds from his inmost being, but it also necessarily proceeds from (and through) his expression, utterance or image. The Power

3. November 1982.
4. See Chapter 8, note 4.
5. 'If the creative artists had been called in to give evidence about the *filioque* clause, they must have come down heavily on the Western side of the controversy, since their experience leaves them in no doubt about the procession of the ghost from the son' (*The Mind of the Maker*, p.139).

flows from the Idea, but only *through* the Activity. Power does not, and will not, proceed directly from the Idea.[6]

The *Filioque*, therefore, is essential to the understanding of the Trinity which the analogy encourages. It was not in the original text because Trinitarian theology had not then reached that degree of definition. Its *absence*, especially an absence long accepted in a particular liturgical tradition, might be consistent with the truth of the doctrine. But its *omission* by those long accustomed to it must inevitably imply that it is wrong or unimportant or meaningless. None of these implications can be tolerated. If the *Filioque* is wrong, then the Spirit is another, or a second, Son. Such a model of the Trinity contradicts the analogy and has no future. As the *Quicunque Vult* rightly observes, there is one Son, not more (v.24), and it is the character of the Spirit to be God in a mode distinct from that of the Father or the Son. If the controversy is meaningless, we are in a worse case still, for that is to say we cannot speak of God in his eternal being, and that is the negation of what this little book has tried to do.

6. See above, Chapters 8 and 9.

Appendix A

Missing Link

In Chapter Seven it was claimed that Dorothy L. Sayers adapted, or shifted, R.C. Moberly's analogy of the Trinity from the human person to the human work, and that she did this by combining it with ideas of human creativity derived, in the immediate instance, from G.K. Chesterton. Her debt to Chesterton and his school cannot be doubted; it is frequently acknowledged. But she never mentions Moberly or shows any conscious knowledge of the passage in *Atonement and Personality*. Did she hit on the analogy independently, or did she know of the Moberly passage, and then subsequently forget or conceal it? As a serious possibility, deliberate concealment may be dismissed. She could have no interest in concealing it; on the contrary, reference to it would have added theological weight and encouraged theologians to take more notice of her work than they did.

There is some circumstantial evidence that she *had* heard

of Moberly's analogy. She was born in Oxford, where her
father, the Rev. Henry Sayers, was Headmaster of Christ
Church Cathedral School at the same time as Moberly was
Canon and Lady Margaret Professor of Divinity. Henry
Sayers certainly instructed his daughter in elementary
Latin (after they moved, in 1898, to Bluntisham-cum-
Earith in Huntingdonshire). Whether he contributed to her
adult views on theology is less certain. But he might well
have made some reference to the Moberly analogy in a
sermon. Or perhaps his brilliant and rebellious daughter
poked fun at the Trinity. She remembered such jokes later,
and gave the devil his due (*The Mind of the Maker*, p.98).
Henry Sayers might have drawn on Moberly in reply,
saying, 'It's not so foolish as you think. Look at it like this
. . .'. Our first encounter with ideas we are subsequently
attached to is often in opposition or rejection.

The recent spate of biographies of Dorothy L. Sayers
might seem to offer hope of detecting the 'missing link' in
the development of the analogy. But Janet Hitchman, in
Such a Strange Lady (New English Library, 1975) mentions
the Trinity only once: 'She, on hearing [a reporter]
approach, had risen to stir the fire. . . . She slewed round,
poker in hand, demanded "Are you a Christian?" and then
proceeded to lecture him for over an hour on the Trinity.'
Serve him right; we can imagine what she said. But it does
not help us with the missing link.

There are two more serious works, Ralph E. Hone,
Dorothy L. Sayers, a Literary Biography (Kent State U.P.,
1979) and James Brabazon, *Dorothy L. Sayers—The Life
of a Courageous Woman* (Gollancz, 1981). They both give
extensive and sympathetic accounts of *The Mind of the
Maker*, but they do not place the analogy in its theological
context, or give us any direct idea where she got it from.

James Brabazon, however, reveals (unconsciously) an
alternative to the 'Henry Sayers' theory. In 1917 Dorothy,
who had obtained the equivalent of a first-class degree
(women were not yet technically admitted as graduates)
and was in Oxford working for Blackwell's, received her
first proposal of marriage. It came from the Vice-Principal
of St. Edmund Hall, the Rev. Leonard Hogdson, and the

couple's acquaintance seems to have ripened in punts on the Cherwell. Hodgson's devotion was not reciprocated and he drops out of the story. But, broken heart or not, he became a noted theologian and ended up as Regius Professor of Divinity and Canon of Christ Church. He published in 1943 *The Doctrine of the Trinity* (Nisbet) which includes a brief and somewhat patronizing notice of *The Mind of the Maker* (p.230). His approach to the doctrine is quite different from that of Sayers, and it contains little that is memorable. But perhaps it was he, rather than Sayers *père*, who passed on the Moberly analogy during those first-war punting parties in Oxford—the academic theologian finding suitable conversation with which to woo a formidable blue-stocking!

We cannot, at the moment, get closer to the missing link than that. By the time Lord Peter Wimsey had had his day and Sayers began to write theology, her version of the analogy was fully developed in her mind and the occasion of her original encounter with it was forgotten. The details of that encounter are of no particular importance for the subject of this book; but we are all detectives now.

Appendix B

The Creeds

(Older translations may be found in the Book of Common Prayer.)

1. The Apostles' Creed

I believe in God, the Father almighty,
creator of heaven and earth.

I believe in Jesus Christ, his only Son, our Lord.
He was conceived by the power of the Holy Spirit
and born of the Virgin Mary.
He suffered under Pontius Pilate,
was crucified, died, and was buried.
He descended to the dead.
On the third day he rose again.
He ascended into heaven,
and is seated at the right hand of the Father.
He will come again to judge the living and the dead.

I believe in the Holy Spirit,
the holy catholic Church,
the communion of saints,
the forgiveness of sins,
the resurrection of the body,
and the life everlasting. Amen.

2. The Nicene Creed

We believe in one God,
the Father, the almighty,
maker of heaven and earth,
of all that is,
seen and unseen.

We believe in one Lord, Jesus Christ,
the only Son of God,
eternally begotten of the Father,
God from God, Light from Light,
true God from true God,
begotten, not made,
of one Being with the Father.
Through him all things were made.
For us men and for our salvation
he came down from heaven;
by the power of the Holy Spirit
he became incarnate of the Virgin Mary, and was made
    man.
For our sake he was crucified under Pontius Pilate;
he suffered death and was buried.
On the third day he rose again
in accordance with the Scriptures;
he ascended into heaven
and is seated at the right hand of the Father.
He will come again in glory
to judge the living and the dead,
and his kingdom will have no end.

We believe in the Holy Spirit,
the Lord, the giver of life,
who proceeds from the Father and the Son.
With the Father and the Son he is worshipped and
    glorified.
He has spoken through the Prophets.
We believe in one holy catholic and apostolic Church.
We acknowledge one baptism for the forgiveness of sins.
We look for the resurrection of the dead,
and the life of the world to come. Amen.

3. *"Quicunque Vult" or Athanasian Creed*

Whosoever would be saved : needeth before all things to hold fast the Catholick Faith.

2 Which Faith except a man keep whole and undefiled : without doubt he will perish eternally.

Now the Catholick Faith is this : that we worship one God in Trinity, and the Trinity in Unity;

4 Neither confusing the Persons : nor dividing the substance.

5 For there is one Person of the Father, another of the Son : another of the Holy Ghost;

6 But the Godhead of the Father, and of the Son, and of the Holy Ghost is all one : the glory equal, the majesty co-eternal.

7 Such as the Father is, such is the Son : and such is the Holy Ghost;

8 The Father uncreated, the Son uncreated : the Holy Ghost uncreated;

9 The Father infinite, the Son infinite : the Holy Ghost infinite.

10 The Father eternal, the Son eternal : the Holy Ghost eternal;

11 And yet there are not three eternals : but one eternal;

12 As also there are not three uncreated, nor three infinites : but one infinite, and one uncreated.

13 So likewise the Father is almighty, the Son almighty : the Holy Ghost almighty;

14 And yet there are not three almighties : but one almighty.

15 So the Father is God, the Son God : the Holy Ghost God;

16 And yet there are not three Gods : but one God.

17 So the Father is Lord, the Son Lord : the Holy Ghost Lord;

18 And yet there are not three Lords : but one Lord.

19 For like as we are compelled by the Christian verity : to confess each Person by himself to be both God and Lord;

20 So are we forbidden by the Catholick Religion : to speak of three Gods or three Lords.

21 The Father is made of none : nor created, nor begotten.

22 The Son is of the Father alone : not made, nor created, but begotten.

23 The Holy Ghost is of the Father and the Son : not made, nor created, nor begotten, but proceeding.

24 There is therefore one Father, not three Fathers; one Son, not three Sons : one Holy Ghost, not three Holy Ghosts.

25 And in this Trinity there is no before or after : no greater or less;

26 But all three Persons are co-eternal together : and co-equal.

27 So that in all ways, as is aforesaid : both the Trinity is to be worshipped in Unity, and the Unity in Trinity.

28 He therefore that would be saved : let him thus think of the Trinity.

Furthermore it is necessary to eternal salvation : that he also believe faithfully the Incarnation of our Lord Jesus Christ.

30 Now the right faith is that we believe and confess : that our Lord Jesus Christ, the Son of God, is both God and man.

31 He is God, of the substance of the Father, begotten before the worlds : and he is man, of the substance of his Mother, born in the world;

32 Perfect God : perfect man, of reasoning soul and human flesh subsisting;

33 Equal to the Father as touching his Godhead : less than the Father as touching his manhood.

34 Who although he be God and man : yet he is not two, but is one Christ;

35 One, however, not by conversion of Godhead into flesh : but by taking manhood into God;

36 One altogether : not by confusion of substance, but by unity of person.

37 For as reasoning soul and flesh is one man : so God and man is one Christ;

38 Who suffered for our salvation : descended into hell, rose again from the dead;

39 Ascended into heaven, sat down at the right hand of the Father : from whence he shall come to judge the quick and the dead.

40 At whose coming all men must rise again with their bodies : and shall give account for their own deeds.

41 And they that have done good will go into life eternal : they that have done evil into eternal fire.

This is the Catholick Faith : which except a man do faithfully and stedfastly believe, he cannot be saved.

Index

Index